How To Know God's Will

First Steps

For The New Christian

S. MAXWELL CODER

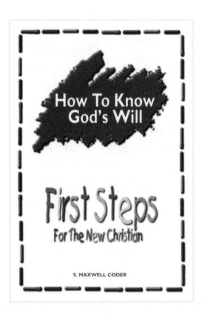

How To Know
God's Will

First Steps
For The New Christian

S. MAXWELL CODER

PRESENTED TO

_____

_____

_____

FROM

_____

_____

_____

MERIDIAN®
PUBLICATIONS

Contents

Preface

To begin to live the Christian life in all its fullness, we must first grasp all that is promised to us and required of us by God's Word, and then begin to apply it.

First Steps for the New Christian — **How To Know God's Will** was initially developed and taught at Moody Bible Institute in Chicago. For over forty years it has been part of a Bible correspondence course for the External Studies Division of Moody Bible Institute.

Now this incisive and insightful book is available for personal or group inductive Bible study to help believers apply the principles of God's Word and come to enjoy the Christian life as God intended it.

How To Know God's Will truly does offer virtually everything you need to know and experience God in your life!

— *The Publisher*

Introduction

"The one who does the will of God abides forever," the Bible says. *How To Know God's Will* guides you into a clear understanding of what the Bible teaches about God's desire for our attitudes and lifestyles as Christians. Designed to be biblical, specific, and practical, this book will also teach you how to begin the journey of discovering God's will for your life.

This book and others in the *First Steps For the New Christian* series provides study materials on the various aspects of living a full, rich Christian life. Other titles in the series currently include:

> *How to Begin Your Christian Life*
> *How to Grow In Your Christian Life*
> *How to Understand Your Bible*

Additional titles in the *First Steps For the New Christian* series are forthcoming.

Because these materials were initially used both as classroom and correspondence school texts, the style is that of a teacher — guiding, challenging, directing, stimulating, and raising questions as well as providing answers.

The content of this edition is taken from an adult credit course from Moody Bible Institute External Studies Division. For information on how you might take this and other courses for credit, write for a free catalog to:

Moody External Studies
Moody Bible Institute
820 North La Salle
Chicago, IL 60610

1

God Has a Plan for Every Life

One of the most practical and inspiring subjects to be found in the Bible is the revelation that God has a plan for every life. When that plan is discovered and followed, it brings greater happiness and success than could be achieved in any other conceivable set of circumstances. This teaching of the Scriptures has a strong appeal to new Christians and to Christian young people with life still before them.

The world knows nothing of the concept of a God-planned life, and for some reason many believers have failed to realize how much of the Bible is devoted to it. As a result, one constantly meets people who have missed the way somewhere. They made wrong choices, over-looked golden opportunities, and finally resigned themselves to a life of unpleasant drudgery or disappointed hopes. Although they would give almost anything to be able to make a fresh start, they know of no way to rectify the mistakes of having planned their own lives and failed.

No instructed Christian needs to fear any such unhappy prospect. God has made us; and he knows our capacities, our weaknesses, our innermost longings and aspirations. He has a divine blueprint for each one of his people, exactly suited to his own peculiar needs, enabling each one to make the most of his possibilities, not only in this life, but also in the life to come. It is easy to discover what it is. In fact, the Lord is more desirous that we learn his plan than we are to learn it. He has made every provision to enable us to follow it. If we have not previously sought to live in accordance with it, we can begin at once, no matter what our age.

The importance of finding God's will is a neglected truth of the Scriptures, but a prominent one. God promises to give us the desires of our hearts if we meet the simple conditions presented in his Word about God's will (Psalm 37:4). Who can remain indifferent in the face of a guarantee like this, backed as it is by the faithfulness of God?

God's Plan Is Reasonable

According to reason, God has a plan for every Christian. Whatever we do, whether we are building a model, making a dress, or playing a game, our minds demand a plan to follow. We turn naturally to a timetable or a road map to travel to a distant point.

Everywhere in the universe, we find intelligent planning. A snowflake or a flower viewed through a microscope shows unmistakable evidence of wonderful design. Our telescopes reveal such a careful arrangement of the movement of the heavenly bodies that we set our watches by them. Every mineral has a purpose. Plants have specific functions to perform—in purifying and perfuming the air, providing food for men and animals, beautifying the earth during life, and enriching the soil in death.

When we reflect that we are the highest of God's earthly creatures, destined for a place in the future even above that of the angels, we must conclude that God has a special work for us to do during our time on earth. He has made us; every talent we possess has come from him; he has purchased us at the cost of his Son's blood. It is unthinkable that he should intend us to live in uncertainty and confusion, with no worthwhile goal to achieve. We are the special objects of his love. We were upon his heart before the world was created (Ephesians 1:4). If he guides the moon, though it is dead and cold, he will surely guide us in such a way as to satisfy every longing he has implanted within us. It is reasonable to believe that we are no exception to the law of creation. God has a purpose for everything in his universe.

SOME EXAMPLES OF GOD-PLANNED LIVES

According to experience, there is a divine plan for each believer. Multitudes of God's people have found his plan for their lives and followed it. For Abraham it meant leaving the city of Ur of the Chaldees and spending the remainder of his years in tents (Hebrews 11:8–10). For Moses it meant giving up the wealth and honor he had

11

enjoyed in Egypt to begin a life of wandering in the wilderness (Hebrews 11:24–27). For David it meant leaving the sheepfold where he had spent his boyhood and sitting on the throne of Israel (1 Chronicles 17:7).

Christian literature furnishes many examples of men and women in every kind of occupation who dedicated their lives to doing God's will. Whether their work was commonplace and obscure, or so unusual as to make them outstanding, they steadfastly walked with God.

Among the more prominent of these may be mentioned Sir Robert Anderson, famous head of Scotland Yard and author of popular books of Bible study. In the business world, the name of Henry P. Crowell stands out as a convincing illustration of what God can do through a man who honors him. Brilliant lawyers like Simon Greenleaf and eminent statesmen like William E. Gladstone are known to history for their zeal in the defense of the faith. Dr. Howard A. Kelly, of Johns Hopkins University, a world-renowned surgeon, was also a noted evangelical believer who sought always to follow Christ. Outstanding scientists like Newton, Faraday, Pasteur, and Fleming tried with all humility to do the Lord's will.

GOD'S PLAN IS TAUGHT IN THE BIBLE

According to revelation, God has a plan for each of us. The Bible's teaching about the subject is vast. Earthly parents may direct the education of their children into paths leading to a lifework that seems desirable, but only God has the infinite wisdom and knowledge needed to guide an individual into the work for which be was endowed at birth. The Lord may, of course, use the prayerful efforts of godly parents to guard their children from mistakes in the choice of a vocation. He also uses our natural inclinations, our environment, and our circumstances.

The personal interest God shows in each one of us, as it is revealed in the Bible, is astonishing. It should lead us to expect to find a rich body of truth about the pathway on which he wants us to walk. The very hairs of our heads are numbered (Matthew 10:30); the Lord knows our sorrows (Exodus 3:7); he records our tears (Psalm 56:8); he takes note of when we sit down and when we rise up (Psalm 139:2); all our thoughts, our ways, and our words are known to him (Psalm 139:2–6); a book of remembrance of those who fear the Lord and think upon his name (Malachi 3:16).

Scattered throughout the Scriptures are many facts about God's program. The Old and New Testaments are in perfect agreement; each provides a wealth of truth about the divine plan.

1. God's plan is personal

Every believer has the right to take the words of Psalm 32:8 (NKJV) as though they were written just for him:

> I will instruct you and teach you in the way you should go; I will guide you with My eye.

An individual pathway is in view, as distinguished from the general way of righteousness set before all Christians.

Three words are used in this verse to tell us how the Lord makes known to us the way in which we are to go. In the Hebrew tongue used by the psalmist, each word is full of meaning. "Instruction" is the enlightening of the intelligence. "Teaching" is the pointing out of a definite course. "Guidance" is the advice needed for particular problems. And notice that God undertakes to do all three for us; he says, "I will."

God's will can become our will. If necessary, God will compel us to follow him. He had to goad Paul as Acts 26:14 (NKJV) shows: "It is hard for you to kick against the goads."

The verse alludes to the ox goad used for keeping oxen subject to their owner's will. God brought Paul into subjection to himself.

2. God's plan is for believers only

In Psalm 32 we find that the promise of guidance is given only to those whose transgressions are forgiven, whose sins are under the blood of Christ, who have made confession to God. No unsaved person has any claim to the promises about a divinely planned life. Instead, the ungodly may be used to reveal God's wrath against sin (Romans 9:22) or, like Nebuchadnezzar, to accomplish the divine purpose in spite of unbelief (Jeremiah 25:9, 12).

The cloud that directed the people of Israel brought nothing but confusion to the Egyptians (Exodus 14:19–20). Before anyone may expect to be led through the wilderness of this world by the modern counterpart of the pillar of fire, he must be sure he is numbered among those to whom the promise is addressed.

> Who is the man that fears the LORD?
> Him shall He teach in the way He chooses
> (Psalm 25:12 NKJV).

3. God's plan is wonderfully detailed

Incredible as such a revelation may seem at first thought, every step we take is "ordered by the LORD" (Psalm 37:23). He does not always reveal the instant future to us, but he does lead each step of the way. Perhaps several paths lie ahead, each one open and inviting; but we need not fear that we shall make a mistake, for it is written:

> In all your ways acknowledge Him,
> And He shall direct your paths
> (Proverbs 3:6 NKJV).

Paul once found himself in a place where he was for a time uncertain about what he should do. When he tried to enter Asia and Bithynia, the Holy Spirit prevented him, and directed him instead to Philippi in Europe (Acts 16:6–10).

What about the multitude of details making up every life? Can God have a purpose in each one? His Word declares in unmistakable terms:

> And we know that all things work together for good
> to those who love God, to them who are the called
> according to his purpose (Romans 8:28).

Furthermore, this verse states that we *know* this is true.

4. God's program is continuous

> The LORD will guide you continually (Isaiah 58:11 NKJV).

His compassions are new every morning. Once he has undertaken to save us, he will never leave or forsake us (Hebrews 13:5). It does not matter whether we are just beginning the Christian life or whether we have long known the Lord, he will guide us every moment if we permit him to do so. He is with us even when we walk through the valley of the shadow (Psalm 23:4).

5. God's program is definite and specific

Your ears shall hear a word behind you, saying, "This
is the way, walk in it,"
Whenever you turn to the right hand
Or whenever you turn to the left (Isaiah 30:21 NKJV).

We may not hear an audible voice today, but it is still true that

The way of the lazy man is like a hedge of thorns,
But the way of the upright is a highway (Proverbs
15:19 NKJV).

What is true of the way of salvation is also true of the divine plan:

Whoever walks the road, although a fool,
Shall not go astray (Isaiah 35:8 NKJV).

6. God's plan allows for special counsel and wisdom

When doubts come as to what we ought to do, we have the privilege of praying for specific directions:

Cause me to know the way in which I should walk,
For I lift up my soul to You" (Psalm 143:8 NKJV;
compare Psalm 27:11).

When we are confronted with particular problems requiring unusual wisdom, the promise of James 1:5 (NKJV) may acquire a new, wonderful meaning; our daily communion with the Lord Jesus will partake of the nature of an important personal consultation.

If any of you lacks wisdom, let him ask of God, who

gives to all liberally and without reproach, and it will be given to him.

The only condition is the realization of our own lack! Whether we are facing an important crisis, or simply doing our daily tasks, we may say with full confidence:

You will guide me with Your counsel,
And afterward receive me to glory
(Psalm 73:24 NKJV).

7. God's plan is sure to be profitable

From the standpoint of present and future advantages alone, the God-planned life is the only wise course to follow. For honoring the Word of God, Joshua was given this guarantee:

For then you will make your way prosperous, and then you will have good success (Joshua 1:8 NKJV).

We have the same promise in Psalm 1:3 (NKJV):

And whatever he does shall prosper.

With so many about us who have failed in what they sought to do, it is wonderful to know that no Christian need fail to accomplish everything God gives him to do, even during hard times (Jeremiah 17:7–8). Not only shall we have prosperity and good success, but we shall have light upon our path (John 8:12), joy in our labors (Acts 20:24), peace in every circumstance (Isaiah 26:3; Philippians 4:7), and satisfaction (Psalm 63:5, 8).

8. God's plan is always good

Ignorance of the Bible may lead some people to speak of God's will as though it were an unavoidable evil. The

Scriptures, on the other hand, speak of "that good, and acceptable, and perfect, will of God" (Romans 12:2). Anyone may prove, or demonstrate, the truth of this by presenting his body to the Lord as a living sacrifice.

9. Obeying God's plan brings assurance

> If any man is willing to do His will, he shall know of the teaching, whether it is of God (John 7:17 NASB).

This is a Bible truth that may be applied to the knowledge of what God would have us to do with our lives, as well as to the knowledge of salvation on receiving Christ (John 6:40). It may be looked upon as a challenge to every Christian to put these things to the test. One reason some believers lack assurance about their relationship to God is that they have been doing their own will, rather than the God's. It is when we do what God wants us to do that we gain the assurance that he is indeed directing our lives.

> These things I have written to you who believe in the name of the Son of God, that you may know that you have eternal life, and that you may continue to believe in the name of the Son of God (1 John 5:13 NKJV).

CONCLUSION

We have seen from reason, from human examples, and from the teaching of the Bible that God has a plan for every Christian's life.

2

Why It Is Important to Know God's Plan

At least seven facts presented in the Scriptures show the importance of learning the plan of God for our lives. They may be applied not only to the specific program of God for each individual but also to the general will of God for all his children, which is a life of constant obedience to his Word. Each of these seven considerations is sufficient in itself to make it imperative that we seriously face the question of what the Lord would have us do.

SEVEN IMPORTANT FACTS

1. We are incapable of planning our own lives

> O LORD, I know the way of man is not in himself;
> It is not in man who walks to direct his own steps
> (Jeremiah 10:23 NKJV).

We lack the capacity to guide our steps correctly. Sin has deprived us of that living contact with God by which he communicates his perfect will to his creatures.

We are sure to go astray unless we learn and follow God's will.

> All we like sheep have gone astray; we have turned,
> every one to his own way (Isaiah 53:6).

Such a statement permits no exceptions; our way is always wrong. The writer of Psalm 119:176 (NKJV), godly as he was, did not hesitate to say to the Lord:

> I have gone astray like a lost sheep;
> Seek Your servant,
> For I do not forget Your commandments.

It is because of what the Lord Jesus did for us on Calvary that our lost communion with God has been restored. When we pray, "Your kingdom come. Your will be done On earth as it is in heaven" (Matthew 6:10 NKJV), we are seeking to conform our lives to God's plan, and we are likewise looking forward to the time when the full results of the cross will be seen on earth, as the prayer, "Your kingdom come," is answered.

2. Only God knows the future

Remember the former things of old: for I am God,

and there is none else; I am God, and there is none
like Me, declaring the end from the beginning, and
from ancient times the things that are not yet done
(Isaiah 46:9–10).

We do not know what lies ahead, but God does; and we
have his reassuring promise:

Thus says the LORD, your Redeemer,
The Holy One of Israel:
"I am the LORD your God,
Who teaches you to profit,
Who leads you by the way you should go
(Isaiah 48:17 NKJV).

If we fail to heed his voice, his sorrowful tones echo in
our hearts:

Oh, that you had heeded My commandments!
Then your peace would have been like a river,
And your righteousness like the waves of the sea
(v. 18 NKJV).

Frequently the Scriptures remind us that our future is
known to God:

For the LORD knows the way of the righteous,
But the way of the ungodly shall perish (Psalm 1:6
NKJV).

In the midst of affliction, Job could say:

He knows the way that I take (Job 23:10 NKJV).

When David was alone among his enemies and hiding
in a cave for safety, he knew the Lord had not forsaken
him, and he wrote:

> When my spirit was overwhelmed within me,
> Then You knew my path (Psalm 142:3 NKJV).

We know not what a day may bring forth (Proverbs 27:1); but when we, like David, dare to believe that God's way is perfect, and trust him to reveal it to us, we can be sure that he will make our way perfect, as he did for David (2 Samuel 22:32–33).

> But the path of the just is as the shining sun,
> That shines ever brighter unto the perfect day
> (Proverbs 4:18 NKJV).

Dark days and uncertainty may sometimes be our experience, but this is anticipated and provided for:

> Who among you fears the LORD?
> Who obeys the voice of His Servant?
> Who walks in darkness
> And has no light?
> Let him trust in the name of the LORD
> And rely upon his God (Isaiah 50:10 NKJV).

3. *The will of God brings lifelong blessings*

Some of these blessings have been mentioned as characteristics of the God-planned life. We shall prosper in the work we undertake, and succeed where others fail. Light, joy, peace, and satisfaction will be ours. We shall be made wiser than our adversaries, and be given understanding beyond that of our teachers, even beyond that of the ancients (Psalm 119:98–100). No fears about the future will cause alarm.

The knowledge of God's will brings new assurance into our prayer life.

> Now this is the confidence that we have in Him, that if we ask anything according to His will, He hears us. And if we know that He hears us, whatever we ask, we know that we have the petitions that we have asked of Him (1 John 5:14–15).

It would be difficult to find a more blessed promise or a greater incentive to learn what it means to pray "according to his will." Obviously, it means that our prayers must be in accord with the Word of God. If a Christian woman insists on marrying an unsaved man in disregard of God's warning about the unequal partnering (2 Corinthians 6:14), she cannot expect God to answer her prayers for happiness. Likewise, the man who does not honor his father and mother, and the father who provokes his son to anger have no right to expect God's blessing on their daily work (Ephesians 6:2–4).

4. The will of God brings blessing in the life to come

> And the world is passing away, and the lust of it; but he who does the will of God abides forever (1 John 2:17 NKJV).

This was the life text of D. L. Moody, and the whole world knows the results of his effort to conform his life to it. He made it his own after hearing the soul-stirring words of his friend, Henry Varley, a Christian businessman: "The world has yet to see what God can do with and for and through and in a man who is fully and wholly yielded to him." Mr. Moody abides forever in glory, and his work abides on earth (John 15:16).

23

Moses lived with the eternal riches in view, which he knew awaited him for obeying God's will:

> Esteeming the reproach of Christ greater riches than the treasures in Egypt; for he looked to the reward (Hebrews 11:26 NKJV).

Abraham, Isaac, and Jacob endured privation as strangers and pilgrims on the earth, for they desired "a better, that is, a heavenly country. Therefore God is not ashamed to be called their God, for He has prepared a city for them" (Hebrews 11:16). Christ exhorted:

> Lay up for yourselves treasures in heaven (Matthew 6:20; 19:21).

The apostle Paul spoke of the rigorous discipline demanded of those who seek to win an athletic contest; then he pointed out how we too must bring our bodies into subjection, if we are to win the highest prize in the heavenly race (1 Corinthians 9:24–27). Just before his death, Paul wrote:

> I have fought the good fight, I have finished the race, I have kept the faith. Henceforth, there is laid up for me the crown of righteousness, which the Lord, the righteous judge, will give to me on that day, and not to me only, but unto all them also that love his appearing (2 Timothy 4:7–8).

5. God wants us to know his will

This is evident from the apostolic prayer of Colossians 1:9:

> "We . . . do not cease to pray for you, and to desire

that [you] might be filled with the knowledge of his
will in all wisdom and spiritual understanding.

A further example of God's interest in our learning of
his will is revealed in his servant Epaphras. Addressing the
Colossian Christians, Paul said:

Epaphras . . . is . . . always laboring fervently for you
in prayers, that you may stand perfect and complete
in all the will of God (Colossians 4:12 NKJV).

The abundant provision God has made for us to discover
his purpose for us indicates how much he desires it.

a. *Prayer* is a part of this provision, as the teaching in
Colossians indicates, and there are other similar references, as in Psalm 27:11 (NKJV):

Teach me Your way, O LORD,
And lead me in a smooth path, because of
my enemies.

b. *The Bible* is likewise a part of the appointed means to
this end.

Your word is a lamp to my feet
And a light to my path" (Psalm 119:105 NKJV).

It has power to keep us from turning aside from the
right way, and to restore us if we have turned aside (Psalm
119:1, 9). When the Word of God is in our hearts, every
step we take is sure and safe (Psalm 37:31), so that we are
able to say:

I delight to do Your will, O my God,
And Your law is within my heart (Psalm 40:8 NKJV).

c. *Every circumstance of our lives* is under the sovereign

control of God. This is an important factor in his making known his program to us. When Joseph was sold as a slave into Egypt, his brothers intended it for evil, but God meant it for good (Genesis 50:20). Saul went out looking for his father's beasts, but he found a kingdom instead (1 Samuel 9 and 10). We may be assured that if we are willing to follow him, the Lord will not permit us to remain ignorant of what he wants us to do with our lives.

6. God commands us to know his will

> Therefore do not be unwise, but understand what the will of the Lord is (Ephesians 5:17 NKJV).

This is just as much a command as "Love one another," "Be holy," "Pray without ceasing," or any other plain statement of Scripture.

It is easier to understand how we are supposed to begin obeying Ephesians 5:17 if we read the preceding verses. In verse 14 is a picture of Christians who are asleep to their privileges and responsibilities. We must wake up and rise to our feet, for we have new life in Christ. We should be giving evidence that we are truly alive in him, unlike those around us who are dead in trespasses and sins (Ephesians 2:1).

When we have done our part, by declaring our purpose to serve Christ, he promises to begin to do things for us. Once we are reborn and standing true for him, the word to us is, "Christ shall give you light." We discern a pathway ahead which his light reveals. The next message is:

> See then that you walk circumspectly, not as fools but as wise (Ephesians 5:15).

> He who is wise wins souls (Proverbs 11: 30 NASB).

A further instruction is given, "redeeming the time, because the days are evil" (Ephesians 5:16). This means make good use of our time, devoting it to Christ, remembering that we are his representatives. Then, having done these necessary things, we shall be able to understand the will of the Lord (v. 17). We shall also be in a position to obey the command, "be filled with the Spirit" (v. 18).

Since we are required to understand the will of the Lord for us, it is obvious that this is an individual, personal matter for each of us.

The Lord may want one person to work in a business office and another to go to the mission field. He may lead one young man to the factory and his brother to the United States Senate.

One young woman will be guided to take up nursing, while her sister will become a wife and mother. The rearing of children for the glory of the Lord is as noble and important a Christian work as any other. Doubtless the mother of the Wesleys did more for the gospel by bringing up her children in the nurture and admonition of the Lord than she could have done as a "Christian worker" in the usual sense of the term.

God makes more people Christian businessmen or tradesmen than pastors and evangelists. It must be remembered that yielding ourselves to God does not necessarily mean agreeing to go to Africa, or entering what is usually called "full-time Christian service," or any other particular kind of work. It does mean offering ourselves to God for whatever life plan he may have chosen for us, even if this requires, as it often does, that we remain right where we are, in the place to which he has already brought us, to be his faithful ambassadors in what may seem to us to be some obscure corner.

7. God commands us to obey his will

As the servants of Christ, doing the will of God from the heart" (Ephesians 6:6).

This commandment to servants of earthly masters ought to send us to prayer and to the study of the Bible to learn God's will for us.

To obey is better than sacrifice,
And to heed than the fat of rams
(1 Samuel 15:22 NKJV).

We ought to obey God rather than men (Acts 5:29).

BEGIN NOW TO FOLLOW GOD'S PLAN

There is a general program to be carried out by all good soldiers of Jesus Christ, and there is also a special program for each one. The Lord has designated the objectives to be achieved by all who serve in his ranks, but he has also given specific objectives to each Christian soldier. If we are trying to follow only the general orders given to everybody who knows Christ, we have missed the fullness of the meaning of Ephesians 6:6, and scores of other passages.

As true believers, we should not neglect any of the Bible's precepts governing the Christian life. The grace of God teaches us that

denying ungodliness and worldly lusts, we should live soberly, righteously, and godly in the present world, looking for that blessed hope and glorious appearing of the great God and our Saviour Jesus Christ (Titus 2:12–13).

But we also want to do the particular job the Lord has assigned to us. If we can finish our course triumphantly, like Paul, we shall find blessing all the way, with rich reward at the end.

The time to begin is right now.

> Forgetting those things which are behind and reaching forth unto those things which are before, I press toward the mark for the prize of the high calling of God in Christ Jesus (Philippians 3:13–14).

If the past has been a failure, the future need not be. Let us obey the exhortation of the apostle Peter who reminds us that, since Christ suffered for us, love and loyalty to him should lead us to devote our lives to him.

> Therefore, since Christ suffered for us in the flesh, arm yourselves also with the same mind, for he who has suffered in the flesh has ceased from sin, that he no longer should live the rest of his time in the flesh for the lusts of men, but for the will of God (1 Peter 4:1–2 NKJV).

3

Important First Steps

Probably most of us suppose we would be quick to obey the Lord if only he would give to us the kind of personal revelation he gave to Elijah or Ezekiel in Old Testament days. Let us not be too quick in saying this, for we may be just as unwilling to serve our Lord. If so, we shall then be in a position to remedy whatever is wrong. The discovery of failure on our part may be the beginning of a life of blessing and success beyond anything we thought could be ours to enjoy.

Almost everyone may have a copy of the Word of God, which reveals his will. If we had to depend on a message of fire written across the sky, or the voice of an angel in a dream, we might easily be deceived. Our memories would not perfectly recall the details or the first impression of such an event. Instead of communicating his program to us by any such method, God has given us his written Word, wonderfully preserved through the ages since it was inscribed by holy men inspired of God.

SOME PERSONAL TESTS

The Bible contains many plain statements about what the Lord would have us do. It also challenges us to test ourselves by what it teaches.

> Examine yourselves whether [you] are in the faith
> (2 Corinthians 13:5).

The original meaning of the language here recalls the method used by ancient assayers to test the purity of gold. They applied a touchstone of jasper or Lydian flint, which revealed whether or not the metal was genuine. Our touchstone is the Word of God. When we apply it to ourselves, comparing what it asks of us with what we find in our own hearts, we learn to what degree we are actually honoring the message of God to us.

There are many explicit statements in the Bible about God's will for his people. We must be ready to show respect for his words:

> The secret of the LORD is with them that fear him; and
> he will [show] them his covenant (Psalm 25:14).

Those who really mean business with God are favored with personal guidance from day to day. Here are four personal tests by which we can determine our willingness to follow the revealed will of God:

1. *Separation from known sin is God's will for us*

> For this is the will of God, even your sanctification
> (1 Thessalonians 4:3).

No one could ask for a plainer statement. Although it is a part of what we have called the general will of God for all his people, it is put in such a way as to supply us with a test case for self-examination.

God is holy. He cannot look on sin with the least degree of allowance.

> If I regard iniquity in my heart, the Lord will not hear
> me (Psalm 66:18).

To cherish some loved sin, refusing to give it up for Christ's sake, is to erect a barrier between us and the blessings of communion with God. If we are serious about learning his plan for our lives, we must consider this verse as one of his first messages to us. He wills that we shall be sanctified.

To be sanctified is to be set apart; this is the meaning of the word. We are set apart unto God, in one sense of the term, the moment we receive Christ, for we are bought with his blood. Some day we shall be set apart from sin forever by being taken to glory with Christ. But 1 Thessalonians 4:3 speaks of our present responsibility. God wants us to take our stand against every form of known sin and to maintain that stand consistently. The context of the verse indicates what kinds of sin are immediately in view: sins of impurity (v. 3); greedy desire for something we do not have (v. 5); and fraud of all kinds, which includes cheating in school examinations just as much as it does the defrauding of others in business (v. 6).

To enable us to become free from such sins, we have

been given the Bible, which sanctifies and cleanses us (Ephesians 5:26). Like a mirror, it shows us our shortcomings and then provides the remedy so that we may be transformed more and more into the likeness of Christ (2 Corinthians 3:18). In addition, the Holy Spirit dwells within us to keep us from giving in to the lusts of the flesh (Galatians 5:16). Also, the Lord Jesus "always lives to make intercession" for all who have come unto God by him (Hebrews 7:25). Everything has been done to make a clean, godly life possible for the Christian.

2. Prayer and thanksgiving are God's will for us

> Pray without ceasing. In everything give thanks; for this is the will of God in Christ Jesus concerning you (1 Thessalonians 5:17–18).

Here is another clear statement, like a voice from heaven answering our question, "Lord, what will you have me do?"

It is a strange thing that, with more books available on the subject than ever before, prayer is almost a lost art. With the riches of the devotional literature of the ages to draw on, people face the most serious kind of trouble without apparently thinking it necessary to spend an hour or two, much less a night, in prayer. It seems almost incredible that we should regard the Word of God so lightly, but it is true.

Pastors frequently find that families have been facing calamities of all kinds, without thinking it necessary to meet with other Christians at a prayer meeting. Missionaries are obliged to face the terrible power of the enemies of the cross without prayer support that could bring down power from on high because so many in the homeland forget that one of the main channels God uses for the blessing of his people is their intercession for one another.

The exhortations, "Pray without ceasing" and "In everything give thanks," mean more than offering an occasional prayer at bedtime or bowing for a moment at lunch. They tell us to lift our hearts to the Lord constantly throughout every day, in thanksgiving for the abundant evidences of his love, and in earnest petition concerning everything we do, that we may please him and have his blessing. We do not have to retire to a monastery to be in communion with the Lord during every waking hour.

> Be anxious for nothing, but in everything by prayer and supplication with thanksgiving let your requests be made known to God. And the peace of God, which surpasses all comprehension, shall guard your hearts and your minds in Christ Jesus (Philippians 4:6–7 NASB).

Perfect peace about the future, as well as about everything else, is dependent on our meeting the threefold requirement calling for *prayer*, which is the ordinary word for continuous communion with God; *supplication,* or the fervent intercession demanded by some situations; and *thanksgiving.* When we remember to do these, we have little difficulty in deciding whether we are where the Lord wants us to be.

3. Good deeds are God's will for us

> For this is the will of God, that by doing good you may put to silence the ignorance of foolish men (1 Peter 2:15 NKJV).

The world is full of ignorant and foolish people who are

quick to make the most of the failings of Christians. We are being watched constantly; therefore, we must be on our guard, quieting the tongues of the enemies of Christianity by deeds of kindness and love. We have no right to give unbelievers ammunition to use against the cause of Christ.

What forms of well doing are in view? The preceding verses afford several suggestions. We are to abstain from fleshly lust. We are to be transparently honest in everything. We are to respect the laws of the land and the rules of the office or shop where we work. This means that we must be careful not to neglect the work for which an employer is paying us, even to engage in Christian service or religious argument. Doubtless we fulfill the spirit of 1 Peter 2:15 when we engage in benevolent enterprises not under the direct control of the church.

> As we have therefore opportunity, let us do good unto all" (Galatians 6:10).

The subject of our good deeds is so important that it is set forth in the Bible as one reason why God has saved us.

> For we are his workmanship, created in Christ Jesus unto good works (Ephesians 2:10).

Christ "gave Himself for us, that He might redeem us from every lawless deed and purify for Himself His own special people, zealous for good works" (Titus 2:14 NKJV).

If we have been neglecting to put good works in their proper place as part of the divine plan for us, we can easily begin at once to bring our lives into conformity with the Word of God. There is an extra incentive in the warning of James 4:17 (NKJV):

> Therefore, to him who knows to do good and does
> not do it, to him it is sin.

The things we fail to do through ignorance are not here in view but the things we know we ought to do and yet neglect. Inactivity then becomes sin.

4. Suffering is sometimes God's will for us

> Therefore let those who suffer according to the will
> of God commit their souls to Him in doing good, as
> to a faithful Creator (1 Peter 4:19 NKJV).

Many examples are found in the Scriptures to show why godly people often suffer.

The three Hebrew young men who were cast into the fiery furnace entered into a new experience of the love of God as the result of their trial. They had a personal revelation of his power to deliver them; they walked with him in the midst of the fire; a divinely given capacity to endure the flame was theirs; the enemies of God were confounded; they became a blessing to multitudes who have read their story (Daniel 3).

It was because the disciples had followed the Lord Jesus into the ship that they found themselves threatened by a terrific storm on the Sea of Galilee (Matthew 8:23–27). He led them into trouble so that they might see the power of his word over the forces of nature.

The blind man in John 9:3 was suffering "that the works of God should be made manifest in him." Because he was born blind, the power of Christ was manifested; both physical and spiritual sight came to him, and the Bible record of his experience has brought many to the Lord.

When Paul was lashed and then thrown into a dungeon

in Philippi, somebody might have said that he was out of the will of God or such a thing could not have happened. Yet he had gone to that city because he obeyed a heavenly vision, given while he was risking his life each day as a foreign missionary. Believers still thank God for the stream of blessing that has flowed from that time of suffering (Acts 16:23–31).

God has a purpose in whatever he permits us to know of affliction.

> If we suffer, we shall also reign with him (2 Timothy 2:12).

If we desire above all else to do God's will, and if it is his purpose that we suffer for a time, let us not complain or rebel but commit ourselves to him as unto a faithful Creator who has a reason for everything he does. He has a perfect plan.

> For whom the Lord loves He chastens,
> And scourges every son whom He receives
> (Hebrews 12:6 NKJV)

He does it for our profit and afterwards it yields "the peaceable fruit of righteousness" (vv. 10–11).

As we pursue the path he sets before us, we are warned in advance about trouble and comforted as well.

> Beloved, do not think it strange concerning the fiery trial which is to try you, as though some strange thing happened to you; but rejoice to the extent that you partake of Christ's sufferings, that when His glory is revealed, you may also be glad with exceeding joy (1 Peter 4:12–13 NKJV).

Reproach and persecution may come. Does this mean we

have missed his plan? Not at all. Rather, if we are re-proached for the name of Christ, it means that "the Spirit of glory and of God" rests upon us (v. 14). This is enough to turn our sorrow into joy. It is a revelation that should make the thorniest part of our pathway a delight.

CONCLUSION

The four personal tests above plainly reveal what the Lord would have us do.

We need to apply the message of 2 Corinthians 13:5 to our lives: "Examine yourselves" Now is the time for you to examine yourselves in the light of the teaching of the Bible. Ask the Lord to enable you to follow the plain instructions of his Word. As you do this, you will have a basis for expecting further guidance in your life (Psalm 25:4).

4

The Steps of a Good Man

No statement of Scripture about the way God leads his people is more startling than Psalm 37:23 (NKJV):

> The steps of a good man are ordered by the Lord,
> And He delights in his way.

Here is a revelation so exceedingly important that it deserves our careful study in the light of its context.

The wonder of this teaching increases when we notice what is really involved. The steps of a good man are *ordered* by the Lord. In the American Standard Version the word is translated *established*. The same Hebrew word is translated ordained in Psalm 8:3 (NKJV), "the moon and the stars, which You have ordained."

The science of astronomy has recorded something of the amazing precision of the movements of the heavenly bodies. Eclipses of the sun and moon, conjunctions of the planets, and other phenomena can be accurately predicted hundreds of years before they occur. A planetarium projects upon a domed screen pictures of the sky that are so perfect that the audience is able to see the stars and planets just as Abraham saw them over the mountains of ancient Canaan, or as they will appear in the distant future. This is possible because God has established a fixed orbit for each heavenly body, which can be calculated with the utmost exactitude.

STEPS ORDERED BY GOD

The same divine wisdom and care that ordained the movements of the stars of the sky also ordained our steps as children of God! The same power by which the stars are kept in their courses is at the disposal of believers to keep them in the way of obedience to the plan of God. This is an astonishing revelation, but it is one that reappears in the New Testament.

> For we are his workmanship, created in Christ Jesus unto good works, which God [has] before ordained that we should walk in them (Ephesians 2:10).

There is a word picture in Jude 13 that presents a striking contrast by describing certain among the ungodly as "wandering stars, to whom is reserved the blackness of darkness for ever." The symbolism is that of a comet, or some other body from outer space, entering the solar system and the warm light of our sun and then departing on a wandering course farther and farther into outer darkness. True believers, on the other hand, are subject to the governing control of the Sun of righteousness (Malachi 4:2). Christ is the center of the divinely chosen orbit in which they move.

Such a disclosure of the interest God shows in his children is far removed from any philosophy of fatalism. It is not as though each believer were a robot, an automaton, acting without any choice of his own. We have been given freedom to accept or to reject the blueprint God offers for the conduct of our lives. A further consideration of Psalm 37 emphasizes this, for not all believers have the right to think of verse 23 as descriptive of them. A clear picture is given of those concerning whom the statement is made.

1. A difficult word

The translation of Psalm 37:23 found in the familiar King James Version of the Scriptures is likely to be misunderstood. We read, "The steps of a *good* man are ordered by the Lord." Notice that the word *good* is printed in italics. This means that it does not appear in the original Hebrew text as written by the psalmist. The great scholars who gave us our King James Version in 1611 were faced with many difficult questions of how best to represent the exact meaning of the Hebrew in our tongue. Where it seemed necessary to add an English word in the interest of clarity or beauty, italics were used to indicate that the word was not found in the original text.

When the translators came to Psalm 37:23, they found an unusual word for man. It has no exact English equivalent. It is used in comparatively few places; in fact, it appears only once previously in the entire book of Psalms:

> O taste and see that the LORD is good: blessed is the man that [trusts] in him (Psalm 34:8).

Its true meaning is established by this first use.

2. "Man" refers to a believer

To say that every good man is under the personal direction of the Lord, is obviously wrong. Among unbelievers there are men the world calls good, but only those who have received Christ are sons of God (John 1:12). The human estimate of goodness is quite different from God's estimate. Our text does not speak merely of any good man, as the world counts goodness. It speaks rather of a believer who is surrendered to the Lord.

One of the very first rules for Bible study is, "Observe the context." That is, we must take into consideration the setting in which we find a verse. A portion of Scripture removed from its place often conveys a meaning quite different from that which was intended.

For example, someone might quote Job 2:4 as a text from the Bible and therefore true:

> All that a man [has] will he give for his life.

However, this is an utterance of Satan, the father of lies; and it is not set forth in the Bible as a true statement at all. Many martyrs have proved that they counted their faith dearer than life itself; many parents have died for the sake of their children.

Psalm 37:23, standing alone, can be misunderstood, since it is only part of an extended description of the faithful people of God. Two men are set over against each other in the context. One is righteous; the other is wicked. One is saved; the other is lost. Even a superficial reading of the entire psalm makes this plain.

FOUR IMPORTANT STEPS

Out of all the truths contained in Psalm 37, four short exhortations in the opening verses may be selected as a description of the individual whose steps are directed by the Lord. These four portions supply us with an easy test for our own self-examination.

1. "Trust in the LORD, and do good" (Psalm 37:3)

Everyone who seeks divine guidance must begin here. The Hebrew word for trusting means to flee for refuge and therefore to have confidence in something. We trust in the Lord when we go to him for refuge from the penalty and power of our sins, to lay hold upon the hope he sets before us (Hebrews 6:18).

Anyone who has confidence in his own goodness, so that he thinks he has earned a certain standing before God, has nothing awaiting him in such a passage as this psalm. The first requirement is trust in the Lord, which means renouncing all trust in self or personal righteousness, to cast oneself upon the mercy and grace of God.

There are many self-righteous persons in the world. When asked about the basis of their hope for heaven, they speak of their success in keeping the Ten Commandments or the Golden Rule. They are doing the best they can; they love their fellow men; they say they are better than some church members they know. Instead of the Bible principle that blood-cleansed sinners go to heaven, they prefer to believe that the "good" go to heaven. Not what Christ has done for them but what they are doing for themselves and others—this is the important thing in their judgment. The words of Ephesians 2:8–9 are overlooked:

> For by grace are [you] saved through faith; and that not of yourselves: it is the gift of God, not of works, lest any man should boast.

"Trust in the LORD, and do good." This is the right kind of goodness, since it springs from sincere trust in Christ. Probably this was what the translators had in mind when they inserted the word "good" in verse 23. Native goodness, sometimes called the milk of human kindness, will not save man. But when someone tries to do good for the sake of Christ, this act becomes an evidence that his faith is genuine. "Faith without works is dead" (James 2:20).

Like other eternal truths revealed in the Old Testament, this one is also found in the New Testament. Paul was commissioned to preach that men "should repent, turn to God, and do works befitting repentance" (Acts 26:20). He wrote:

> I want you to affirm constantly, that those who have believed in God should be careful to maintain good works (Titus 3:8).

We cannot separate faith from good works, as though one could be independent of the other. Good works are a natural outcome of faith.

2. Delight yourself also in the Lord, And He shall give you the desires of your heart (Psalm 37:4 NKJV)

Here is something that follows salvation by faith in Christ. It is a second step not yet taken by every believer.

All Christians have trusted in the Lord but not all have delighted in the one whom they have trusted; and the fact that they do not have the desires of their hearts is proof of this.

What a promise this is! Every desire will be granted to us by the Lord, if we fulfill the single condition mentioned. The fault lies with us alone if this is not our own daily experience. God has never failed to keep his word, he will honor it when we grant to him our implicit obedience.

Some delight in pleasure. Others find their chief delight in business, or a career, or music, or fishing, or any one of a thousand other things. Obviously, many of these are good and profitable, each in its proper place. God has given all the world, brimful of wholesome pleasures, richly for us to enjoy (1 Timothy 6:17). It is only when something usurps the place rightfully belonging to him that it becomes sin.

It is not difficult to learn what it means to delight ourselves in the Lord. It is to live so as to please him, to honor everything in his Word, to do everything in the way he would like to have it done, and for him.

The concept of delight is found in another passage addressed to Israel, where its meaning is made clear:

> If you turn away your foot from the Sabbath,
> From doing your pleasure on My holy day,
> And call the Sabbath a delight,
> The holy day of the Lord honorable,
> And shall honor Him, not doing your own ways,
> Nor finding your own pleasure,
> Nor speaking your own words,
> Then you shall delight yourself in the Lord;

And I will cause you to ride on the high hills of
the earth,
And feed you with the heritage of Jacob your father.
The mouth of the Lord has spoken (Isaiah 58:13–14
NKJV).

Delighting to obey the Lord is the same thing as delighting in the Lord himself. The principle found in this passage may be applied to any other command of the Bible. If we delight in having no other gods before him, delight in honoring our fathers and mothers, delight in keeping all the teachings of Scripture, we shall be delighting ourselves in him. "Those who honor Me I will honor" (1 Samuel 2:30). This is a law of the spiritual world. If we want to ride upon the high places of the earth, knowing heaven's highest blessings in the fulfillment of the desires of our hearts, here is the secret. We must respect the Scriptures enough to make them our rule of life.

3. *"Commit your way to the Lord,*
Trust also in Him,
And He shall bring it to pass" (Psalm 37:5 NKJV)

It is fitting that this should be the third admonition of the psalm, because it belongs after the others. Not until we have trusted in Christ as Savior, then delighted ourselves in him as Lord, does he speak about taking charge of us and leading us into the fullness of his blessing.

If we have not trusted in him, we are not yet children of God at all. If we have not delighted ourselves in him, we have not taken our salvation very seriously, and it is doubtful that we would respond to the guidance he yearns to provide. As long as our own way is so pleasant that we delight in it rather than in him, we shall not be ready to take the third logical step toward walking in his path.

There is a word picture here. To "commit" is to act like a man who, carrying a burden he is unable to bear, rolls it on the shoulders of someone stronger than he is, one who is willing to carry his load for him. When we commit our way unto the Lord, we acknowledge that this is our situation. We tell him we cannot guide our own lives correctly, and we entrust them to him as the one who is able and willing to take complete charge of them.

The remainder of the verse is not to be overlooked. Having completed the act of committing our way unto the Lord, we are to begin a process of continuous trust. Our part in the transaction is not finished when we have decided we want the Lord to direct our steps and have told him so at some dedication service.

Necessary as the act of commitment is, it must be followed by obedience to the further words, "Trust also in him." We are to keep on trusting, even though the promised response may seem long in coming from the Lord. It may take a long time for him to bring us to the place where we shall be aware of his all-wise guidance. By trusting in him throughout such a period of necessary heart preparation, we give evidence of the sincerity of our declaration. The reward of faith is sure: "He shall bring it to pass." God will do what he has promised. He will vindicate his people who have dared to trust him. Their righteousness and their judgment will someday be recognized by all.

4. "Rest in the Lord, and wait patiently for Him" (Psalm 37:7)

Resting in the Lord means refraining from anxious thought about the future (Matthew 6:34).

But the wicked are like the troubled sea,
When it cannot rest" (Isaiah 57:20 NKJV).

On the contrary, the prophet addressed the Lord, saying:

You will keep him in perfect peace,
Whose mind is stayed on You,
Because he trusts in You (Isaiah 26:3 NKJV).

It is not always easy to decide what God's plan is. Having told him by acts and words that we mean business with him, we are to rest quietly in full confidence that he will make the way plain. It is not necessary to jump hastily through the first door that seems to be open.

Verse 34 (NKJV) continues the thought:

Wait on the Lord,
And keep His way,
And He shall exalt you. . . .

Our true exaltation will take place at his coming, of course, but he will often exalt us in this present life.

Humble yourselves therefore under the mighty hand of God, that he may exalt you in due time: casting all your care upon him, for he [cares] for you (1 Peter 5:6–7).

Open reward is given for secret prayer (Matthew 6:6).

Let us suppose we have been trying to obey the four admonitions found at the beginning of Psalm 37, after carefully considering what they mean. But we are conscious of our own weakness, and we hesitate to believe that such a wonderful revelation can be true of us, that our steps are established by the Lord in an ordained path.

We know we have been guilty of unworthy thoughts, words, and acts. Does not our failure to be all the Lord would have us to be exclude us from the promise? The wonderful answer is that the verses that follow recognize human frailty and infirmity as an element in our walk and make provision for it.

THE RESULT OF PROPER STEPS

It is written about the trusting, obedient individual described in this psalm that the Lord

> delights in his way.
> Though he fall, he shall not be utterly cast down;
> For the Lord upholds him with His hand"
> (37: 23–24 NKJV).

This is language we all can understand. God rejoices in the way we take. When we stumble, like children learning their first steps, he puts us on our feet again. We have seen earthly parents delighting in the efforts being made by their children to walk after their example. The father holds the hand of his small son to guide him. The child is weak. When he stumbles and loses his balance for a moment, he does not come to any serious harm because a stronger hand than his is holding him.

God is our heavenly Father. He watches our steps with great interest and tender compassion. When we fall, in our weakness, he gently restores us to our place so that we are not utterly cast down. Stern measures may sometimes be required, if we repeatedly demand our own way; but if our delight is in him (v. 4), then his delight is in us (v. 23).

Thus, our weakness and God's strength are found linked together in what the Bible teaches about his program for our lives. Our tendency to fall is met with his desire to lead us by the hand.

> If I take the wings of the morning,
> And dwell in the uttermost parts of the sea,
> Even there Your hand shall lead me,
> And Your right hand shall hold me (Psalm 139:9–10 NKJV).

The Lord Jesus said of his own:

> My Father, which gave them me, is greater than all; and man is able to pluck them out of my Father's hand (John 10:29).

David wrote Psalm 37 after a long life, during which he had ample opportunity to observe God's people. He said:

> I have been young, and now am old; yet have I not seen the righteous forsaken, nor his seed begging bread (v. 25).

Trials will surely come to us, but our trust is in the Lord. He is our strength in time of trouble (v. 39). He will guide us through every circumstance until we have finished our earthly course.

5

*T*he *Threefold Rule of Earth's Wisest Man*

Solomon has always been famous for his wisdom. He wrote the book of Proverbs, the most remarkable collection of wise sayings in all literature. When his fame began to spread over the whole earth, the Queen of Sheba proved him with hard questions. Her judgment was, "the half was not told me. Your wisdom and prosperity exceed the fame of which I heard" (1 Kings 10:7 NKJV).

PROVERBS, A BOOK OF WISDOM

The older we get, the more we realize the truth of this position. The Proverbs exceed anything we have ever heard about them because they are crystallized wisdom of the wisest man who ever lived. When King Solomon was offered his heart's desire by the Lord, he set riches and honor aside to ask in all humility:

> Give to Your servant an understanding heart to judge Your people, that I may discern between good and evil (1 Kings 3:9 NKJV).

The gracious response came:

> Behold, I have done according to your words; see, I have given you a wise and understanding heart, so that there has not been anyone like you before you, nor shall any like you arise after you (v. 12 NKJV).

The book of Proverbs is God's wisdom communicated to his people to govern their lives on the earth. Great men of God in every generation have borne witness to the truth that when they conducted their affairs on the principles set forth in this book, they prospered beyond their expectations. Notable examples of this are known in our own day, and this will continue to be the case until the Lord comes.

1. It is helpful for young Christians

It is to be expected that such a book should contain explicit directions by which new Christians and young people can determine God's will for them. The very language of Proverbs seems to have been chosen with them in mind. The first seven chapters are plentifully sprinkled with verses that begin with the words, "My son." Most of these chapters open with this form of address, making us feel that God the Father is speaking directly to us as his children. No better advice could be given to young Christians faced with the wonderful possibilities that life presents than this: make the reading of Proverbs a daily habit.

2. It puts first things first

On the threshold of the book is one of the key phrases to the understanding of the plan of God:

> The fear of the LORD is the beginning of knowledge (Proverbs 1:7).

Of those who refuse this revelation, it is written:

> Because they hated knowledge
> And did not choose the fear of the Lord,
> They would have none of my counsel
> And despised my every rebuke.
> Therefore they shall eat the fruit of their own way,
> And be filled to the full with their own fancies.
> (Proverbs 1:29–31 NKJV).

It was because people wanted their own way that Christ had to die on the cross (Isaiah 53:6). It is because people want their own way that they live unhappy, defeated lives.

3. It promises God's guidance

Solomon had a great deal to say about right and wrong paths and the blessing God sends to those who follow where he leads. One statement stands out as a marvel of simplicity and comprehensiveness. It is given the central position among five very practical rules of life found in Proverbs 3:1–10. Each of these is worthy of careful attention.

Long life and peace are promised to those who forget not the law of God but keep his commandments from the heart (vv. 1–2). Favor and good understanding in the sight of God and man are the sure portion of those who are characterized by mercy and truth (vv. 3–4). God's guidance is given to those who fully trust him rather than their own human wisdom (vv. 5–6). Health and strength accompany a humble fear of God (vv. 7–8). Temporal prosperity is offered to all who honor the Lord with their substance (vv. 9–10).

Someone may be inclined to ask after years of sincere effort to respect these precepts, "Why do I yet suffer affliction?" The answer is found in the verses that follow. When God the Father chastens his children, he does it in tender love:

> My son, do not despise the chastening of the Lord,
> Nor detest His correction;
> For whom the Lord loves He corrects,
> Just as a father the son in whom he delights (vv. 11–12 NKJV).

It is *because* we are seeking to obey these rules of life that our Father takes charge of us. His care includes such discipline as we may need to prepare us for future service on earth as well as for the high place he wants us to occupy in eternity.

THREE BASIC RULES FOR GUIDANCE

The matchless words of Solomon about divine guid-

ance, found enshrined in the very heart of this section of
the Proverbs, call for careful consideration:

> Trust in the Lord with all your heart,
> And lean not on your own understanding;
> In all your ways acknowledge Him,
> And He shall direct your paths (vv. 5–6 NKJV).

Three conditions for us to meet are set forth here: the
first and last are positive and have to do with our relationship to the Lord; the central one is negative and has to do
with us.

1. "Trust in the Lord with all your heart"

We found this same precept at the beginning of Psalm
37:3, but an important phrase is added, "with all your
heart." We know what it is to trust in the Lord if we are
Christians. Every believer has already obeyed the first four
words of the verse. But it cannot be said that every believer
has obeyed the entire first phrase, by trusting with all his
heart.

This becomes apparent when we observe that this whole
section is addressed to those who are already children of
God by faith. Otherwise we cannot understand it. Unbelievers are never told to honor the Lord with their substance (v. 9). Instead,

> The sacrifice of the wicked is an abomination to the
> LORD, but the prayer of the upright is his delight
> (15:8).

Nor does the Bible ever speak of the unsaved as sons of
the Father, whom he corrects because he loves them (v.
12). Rather, some are called "the children of the wicked

one" (Matthew 13:38), whose father is the devil (John 8:44).

We are required by these considerations to look upon Proverbs 3:5 as a message to believers, calling on them to carry their trust to the point where it takes possession of their hearts. The first and great commandment of the law was:

> You shall love the Lord your God with all your heart (Matthew 22:37 NKJV).

The first rule for knowing God's plan for our lives is that we trust him with all our hearts.

Such a command is reasonable enough, for any lack of confidence in him would keep us from entering wholeheartedly into his program. When a ship enters the difficult waters leading to some great inland port, the captain surrenders all control of his vessel to the pilot who knows the way ahead. There must be perfect trust in the pilot's ability. When we go to a strange city and engage a taxicab to take us through the maze of streets to our destination, we trust ourselves altogether to the driver's knowledge of the way. It would be folly to do otherwise. Likewise, we must be willing to let God take full charge of us.

It must be realized that we cannot reserve any right of self-will in any matter whatsoever. God's will is best. He has placed all the riches of his wisdom, power, and love at our disposal. Therefore, we have no reason for being concerned about the future.

Sometimes Christians trust the Lord up to a certain point, but they become frightened when the pathway seems to get dark. He will fulfill all his Word. When we cleave to the Lord with purpose of heart, he responds in such a way as to exceed our expectations, often after the period of testing has ended.

2. *"Lean not on your own understanding"*

Trust in the Lord must not only be entire; it must be exclusive as well. As soon as we trust in ourselves, we show that our hearts have departed from the Lord (Jeremiah 17:5). There is no room for confidence in the flesh in the life of faith. Human understanding has been darkened ever since sin came into the world (Ephesians 4:18). It is not a dependable guide apart from God.

This warning against human understanding does not mean that there is no place for the intelligent exercise of good judgment. There are many precepts regarding the cultivation of understanding (Proverbs 2:3; 4:7). Christ opened the understanding of his disciples on the resurrection day (Luke 24:45). Paul prayed that the Ephesian Christians might have more understanding (Ephesians 1:18). However, the teaching of Proverbs 3:5 is that we should not depend solely upon this human faculty.

There may be two courses of action open to us. One of them appears to be very desirable. It has advantages that are easy to see. The other one presents difficulties and may even involve hardship; but it is in keeping with the plain teaching of the Bible, while the other is not.

Then we must not—we dare not—do what our unenlightened understanding may dictate. We must do what the Word of God indicates is best for us spiritually, no matter how attractive something else may seem temporarily. We cannot see ahead, but the Lord can. We do not know all the factors; he does. He will vindicate our course later if we trust him and refuse to lean on our own judgment apart from his Word.

A young man with a beautiful voice, which he was using for the Lord on the radio, was offered a position in Hollywood, where his talents would have brought him a large income and great popularity. Knowing that to accept would mean using his voice for worldly gain in a questionable enterprise and at the price of setting a bad example for other young Christians, he refused. There can be no doubt that he did the right thing, as judged by the Bible and in view of eternity. The world would count him foolish now, but the day will come when the whole universe will know that he was wise. In the meanwhile, he has a satisfaction that money can never buy.

A difficult problem facing young people in high school is the question of which college to attend. The choice may be between a famous center of learning and culture, where infidel teachers scoff at the Bible, and a small college where the faculty is made up of men of God. Human understanding might favor the big university because of the high rating it gives its graduates, but this must not be made the sole consideration. In pagan universities, some young people have been known to lose their "faith," while others have emerged the stronger for their contacts with unbelief and new points of view. A decision to attend such an institution should not be made until it is certain that one is sufficiently well-grounded in the Word of God to be beyond the reach of skeptics and the specious claims of false theories.

Intelligent faith has nothing to fear from scientific facts, but there is danger when a young person who has had no real understanding of Bible truth receives his education from men who take every opportunity to attack the Scriptures. It need hardly be said that the presence of scoffers in some colleges should not result in a lowering of the educational standards of evangelical Christians. God places no premium on ignorance. His Word admonishes us to gain knowledge and wisdom with diligence (Proverbs 4:5–9; 22:29). Our testimony carries more weight when we have done this by carefully preparing ourselves.

Leaning on an unenlightened understanding is quite different from the prayerful use of the faculties God has given us to determine his will. He never asks us to abandon all sound judgment. When we are subject to his Word, our understanding is illumined so that it recognizes the wisdom of his plan as it unfolds, and we give our intelligent approval. Human vision is shortsighted. Outward appearances are not always encouraging, but the Lord wants us to have quiet assurance and peace, no matter bow dark the future may seem (Isaiah 32:17).

3. "In all your ways acknowledge Him"

This is a familiar thought to every Christian. There are four ways in which we can acknowledge him. The first is by confessing him before others.

> Therefore whoever confesses Me before men, him I will also confess before My Father who is in heaven (Matthew 10:32 NKJV).

> If you confess with your mouth the Lord Jesus and believe in your heart that God has raised Him from the dead, you will be saved (Romans 10:9 NKJV).

These verses speak of the present assurance and future destiny of those who acknowledge Christ as Savior. Proverbs 3:6, on the other hand, speaks of the continuous guidance provided for those who acknowledge him in all their ways as they try to serve him in everyday life.

We are thus confessing him when we tell others how we received him as Savior. This does not mean talking about him in an ostentatious way wherever we happen to be. We do not have to carry a banner on a stick through a crowded city street to be faithful representatives of Christ; nor is it necessary for us to force ourselves on those we meet. He will give us opportunities to speak to hearts he has already prepared if we make this a matter of definite, daily prayer.

A second way to acknowledge him is to show by actions and words what he has come to mean to us. The world is able to see whether we are bearing the fruit of the spirit—"love, joy, peace, longsuffering, kindness, good-ness, faithfulness, gentleness, self-control" (Galatians 5:22–23). People notice it when we refuse to have any part in things a Christian should not do. The way we live, the places we go, the company we keep, all form a part of our public witness for the Lord. These alone, however, are hardly sufficient if we remain silent when Christ needs a true witness, whether it be in reproach of sin or in the positive affirmation of the gospel.

A third way to acknowledge him is to carry his fragrance in our lives. Those who work with aromatic wood carry the perfume with them unconsciously wherever they go. In the days of the early disciples, others "realized that they had been with Jesus" (Acts 4:13). This ought to be true of us, not because of any boasting display of sanctity, but because the fragrance of the Lord Jesus permeates every-thing we do, since we are so much in his presence.

Finally, we are acknowledging the Lord when we go to him for counsel about all our ways. Every step is to be taken under his direction. His wisdom ought to guide us even in small matters. He loves to be consulted by those who trust him. We are not to suppose that any circumstance is so clear as to make this unnecessary. Even Joshua made a serious mistake when he "did not ask counsel of the LORD" in the matter of the Gibeonites (Joshua 9:14). Whether the way be clear or dark, we are to acknowledge our dependence upon him.

THE RESULT OF OBEDIENCE

These are the three simple rules given by God through Solomon as the secret of divine guidance. Other Scripture passages elaborate upon them, but these three principles are fundamental. When we observe them in all sincerity, we have the guarantee, "He shall direct [our] paths." The Lord will take full charge of us. The promise could not be more specific.

If we are not at the moment in the place he wants us to be, we may rest assured that he will lead us out of our present position into the place of his choosing. In the meantime, "Let each one remain in the same calling in which he was called" (1 Corinthians 7:20 NKJV). In God's own time, when he sees that we are ready, he will lead us into the work he wants us to do for him.

6

An Example to Follow

The life of the Lord Jesus Christ presents us with a perfect illustration of absolute conformity to the will of God. We are not likely to realize how important a place this is given in the record of his ministry until we bring together a number of Scripture passages devoted to it. No study of the God-planned life would be complete without some reference to the way it was exemplified in the Lord Jesus.

CHRIST IS A PERFECT EXAMPLE

When Peter wrote of the Lord as our example, he used a remarkable word found nowhere else in the Bible.

> For to this you were called, because Christ also suf-
> fered for us, leaving us an example, that you should
> follow His steps (1 Peter 2:21 NKJV).

In the Greek language "example" was *hypogrammos*, an expression familiar enough to the schoolrooms of ancient Greece. It was the line of script placed at the top of a page for the children to copy in their writing exercises. It contained all the letters of the alphabet, providing a perfect standard by which the work of each child could be guided and judged. Similar copybooks, with samples of beautiful English script, were once used in American schoolrooms. It teaches us that we are to be like school children in our relationship to Christ. He is our example; we are to reproduce his character before the world.

When we receive him as Savior, the fresh open page of the future lies before us. It is our happy task to show forth his grace and sweetness and love to those about us.

At first we are "babes in Christ" (1 Corinthians 3:1). But soon we begin to grow in knowledge (2 Peter 3:18), in obedience to the command, "as newborn babes, desire the pure milk of the word, that you may grow thereby" (1 Peter 2:2 NKJV). We become "wise for salvation" (2 Timothy 3:15), and normally we become more Christ-like.

When we have finally reached the bottom of the page of our earthly lives, we should be giving evidence that we have kept our example before us always, "for to this you were called" (1 Peter 2:21 NKJV).

CHRIST AND THE WILL OF GOD

Every Bible teaching about the Christian life finds in the Lord Jesus its perfect embodiment. For example, in him we learn about prayer and love and holiness. He illustrates undeviating conformity to the will of the Father. No matter where we look, we find him entirely subject to the divine program.

1. In his life purpose

One of the plainest revelations about the object for which the Lord left glory and came to earth is found in his discourse on the bread of life:

> For I have come down from heaven, not to do My own will, but the will of Him who sent Me (John 6:38 NKJV).

A much earlier statement appears in Hebrews 10:5–10 (NKJV; compare Psalm 40:6–8). It begins with the astonishing words, "when He came into the world, He said:

> Sacrifice and offering You did not desire,
> But a body You have prepared for Me.

Every effort to get rid of the plain meaning of this verse, by those who deny the pre-existence and the deity of our Lord, has failed. The eternal Son of God came into the world in fulfillment of this and many other Old Testament prophecies.

Now the subject of this conversation between God the Father and God the Son was the purpose the Son was to accomplish with the body prepared for him. Throughout the history of the human race, burnt offerings and sacrifices for sin had been offered, but these could not cancel sin (Hebrews 10:3–6). Then Christ came; and he could say in very truth:

Behold, I have come—In the volume of the book it is
written of Me—To do Your will, O God (v. 7 NKJV).

What was the nature of God's will for his Son? The
answer is found in verse 10 (NKJV):

By that will we have been sanctified through the
offering of the body of Jesus Christ once for all.

He was born to die. Through his death we are set apart to
God.

There is a definite parallel between Christ and those
who follow him. We, too, have the privilege of knowing
that we are to fulfill an eternal destiny, having been
"predestined according to the purpose of Him who works
all things according to the counsel of His will" (Ephesians
1:11). The word *predestinated* simply means that our destiny has been determined beforehand by the God who has
called us according to his purpose. He foreknew everything about us, including the fact that we would receive
his Son as our Savior (Romans 8:28–29).

We open the Bible and read, "He chose us in Him before
the foundation of the world" (Ephesians 1:4 NKJV); or,
"God from the beginning chose you for salvation"
(2 Thessalonians 2:13 NKJV). It is a source of wonder and
inspiration to learn these things. Our only fitting response
is to echo the words of Christ our example:

I delight to do Your will, O my God (Psalm 40:8 NKJV).

2. *In the days of his youth*

The Scriptures reveal but one incident in the life of the
Lord Jesus during the thirty years between his early child-
hood and the opening of his public ministry. Yet that

single reference contains evidence that even as a boy Jesus was doing his Father's will.

When Jesus was twelve years old, Joseph and Mary found him in the Temple at Jerusalem among the doctors of the law. Questioned about what he had been doing, he replied:

> Did you not know that I must be about My Father's business? (Luke 2:49 NKJV).

One of the reasons why this story has been included in the brief New Testament record of the life of Christ is its value as a testimony to young people. People can live as the Father would have them live, even during school days. Indeed, God's Word says:

> Remember now your Creator in the days of your youth (Ecclesiastes 12:1 NKJV).

3. In every relationship

In relation *to the Scriptures,* the Lord Jesus esteemed the words of the Father more than his necessary food. When his disciples wondered how he could be more interested in winning a lost soul than in refreshing his body when hungry, he said:

> My food is to do the will of Him who sent Me, and to finish His work (John 4:34 NKJV).

In *relation to others,* Christ placed those who do God's will on a higher plane than his earthly brothers, sisters, and mother. The new relationship existing between him and all who respect the Word of God as he did, is so real, so important, that it goes far beyond anything known by those who had been brought up under the same roof with him in Nazareth.

> For whoever does the will of My Father in heaven is
> My brother and sister and mother" (Matthew 12:50
> NKJV; compare Mark 6:3).

This brings him very close to all of us; it promises a communion with him of surpassing satisfaction and joy.

In *relation to prayer,* the Lord sought nothing outside the purpose for which God had sent him. We are taught by him to pray:

> Your will be done
> On earth as it is in heaven (Matthew 6:10 NKJV).

Such a petition implies willingness to do our part in bringing about that for which we pray. It includes the thought, "Your will be done in me." Active obedience is something quite different from the mere repetition of a prayer that is not really understood.

> Not everyone who says to Me, "Lord, Lord," shall
> enter the kingdom of heaven, but he who does the
> will of My Father in heaven (Matthew 7:21).

In *relation to the* kingdom *of God.* Christ taught that the kingdom of God is made up of those who are willingly subject to his will. To illustrate, he used the parable of the two sons. One actually obeyed his father, and one did not, despite the best of intentions (Matthew 21:28–32). When people with a background of sin and rebellion against God repent and do his will, as the first son and "tax collectors and harlots" (Matthew 21:31) did, they go into the kingdom of God, while the willful, self-righteous remain outside. The Father's will is that all who honor the word of his Son shall have everlasting life "in the kingdom of their Father" (Matthew 13:43; compare John 6:39–40).

4. *In words and deeds*

The Lord Jesus never said one word that came from his own will as separate from the Father's. He said:

> My doctrine is not mine, but his that sent me (John 7:16).

> The word which you hear is not Mine but the Father's (John 14:24 NKJV).

We must learn that our tongues need to be controlled by the Holy Spirit (James 3:6). If we follow Christ's example in this, we shall be guilty of "neither filthiness, nor foolish talking, nor coarse jesting" (Ephesians 5:4), which are three expressions denoting any form of speech that tends toward sin. God is able to set a guard over our mouths and to keep watch over the door of our lips (Psalm 141:3).

Christ never did anything apart from the Father. His deeds were the works that the Father had given him to finish (John 5:36). In fact, he said:

> I do nothing of Myself; but as My Father taught Me (John 8:28 NKJV).

In like manner, all our actions are governed by the command:

> And whatever you do in word or deed, do all in the name of the Lord Jesus, giving thanks to God the Father through Him (Colossians 3:17 NKJV).

For Christ, this meant the renunciation of all self-will

and all seeking for his own glory. It means no less for us. He has given the example:

> I do not seek My own will but the will of the Father who sent Me (John 5:30 NKJV).

> I do not seek My own glory (John 8:50 NKJV).

To follow him in this means rich gain, rather than loss. It brings to us something of the joy of communion with the Father that Christ knew. He could say:

> The Father [has] not left me alone, for I do always those things that please him (John 8:29; compare 16:32).

Nor will God leave us alone if we strive to please him. The planned pathway is never a lonely one, so far as fellowship with the Lord is concerned.

> If [anyone loves] me, he will keep my words; and my Father will love him, and we will come unto him, and make our abode with him (John 14:23).

5. In suffering and death

Peter's reference to Christ as our example is placed in a section of his epistle dealing with suffering. It is followed by two references to believers' suffering according to the will of God (1 Peter 3:17; 4:19). We are said to be "partakers of Christ's sufferings" because we are members of his body, and we live in a world which crucified him and is antagonistic to all who belong to him (John 16:33).

In Christ we find the proper Christian attitude toward affliction. Although his holy nature shrank from the dreadful prospect, he had devoted himself to becoming sin for us and was prepared to endure this terrible mission regardless of the cost. His prayer in Gethsemane was:

> Father, if it is Your will, take this cup away from Me; nevertheless not My will, but Yours, be done (Luke 22:42 NKJV).

This must sometimes be our own prayer. If God will, he is able to deliver us from impending trouble; but if not, we know his will is best. That which has been planned and permitted by divine love and wisdom should be acceptable to us. A good example of how we ought to regard trying circumstances is found in Daniel 3:17–18.

When Christ was born, a definite program lay before him. Throughout his life, he labored to "finish His work" (John 4:34; 5:36). The moment at last arrived when the end of his life on earth was in sight. He was nailed to the cross. As the whole prophetic outline of his earthly ministry came before him on Calvary, he knew that Psalm 69:21 still awaited fulfillment:

> And [for] my thirst they gave me vinegar to drink.

Vinegar had been offered to him once, but before the burning thirst of crucifixion was upon him (Matthew 27:34). Parched at last with thirst, Jesus, knowing that all things were now accomplished, that the scripture might be fulfilled, [said], "I thirst!" (John 19:28). His regard for the Scriptures continued to the end. The agony of Calvary did not cause him to forget for a moment his purpose to do God's perfect will.

It was when Jesus had received the vinegar that he said, "It is finished!" And he bowed his head, and gave up his spirit. Much has been written about what was finished at his death. Our salvation was an accomplished fact; its righteous basis was now provided. Satan's defeat was sure; the power of sin was broken. But the thing of importance to our study is that Christ fulfilled God's will by finishing what he had come to do. An example was now set before the people of God wherein they could see embodied everything written about the God-planned life.

How this applies to us

In Christ we see perfectly exemplified the four statements from the Scriptures by which our willingness to follow can be tested. Christ was separate from sin; he prayed without ceasing; he went about doing good; he suffered according to the will of God (see chapter 3). He illustrated the precepts of Psalm 37 by trusting in the Father, delighting himself in him, committing his way unto him, and resting in him (chapter 4). He personified the wisdom of Solomon by trusting the Father with all his heart, leaning not unto his own understanding, and acknowledging him in all his ways (chapter 5).

The fact that the Lord Jesus is the only Person who has ever perfectly done God's will from birth to death does not in any sense lessen the value of the things we observe in his life. The revelation that he did all these things without sin, having no inborn tendency to self-will, does not make his example any less useful to us. In fact, it is through him, and through him only, that we have hope of walking well pleasing to God. He dwells in our hearts by faith. He enables us by his gracious Spirit, by the power he supplies, to face the future, knowing that it is possible for us faithfully to carry out God's program for our own lives.

7

Important New Testament Teachings

Many passages in the New Testament deal with the will of God. A few of these have already been noticed, since they were anticipated in the Old Testament. These New Testament passages illustrate important general principles having to do with the God-planned life. From these general principles we can develop specific rules for discovering the divine program for each of us.

1. *We do not know the future*

When Paul sailed from Ephesus, he said to his friends:

> I will return again unto you, if God will (Acts 18:21).

It was his desire at another time to go to Corinth and help the church there, but his plans were made subject to his Lord's program. Therefore, he wrote:

> I will come to you shortly, if the Lord will (1 Corinthians 4:19).

Again, he said:

> I hope to stay a while with you, if the Lord permits (1 Corinthians 16:7 NKJV).

The same restraint is to be seen in his epistle to the church at Rome (Romans 1:10; 15:32).

We have no more right than Paul to declare in the presence of others that it is God's will for us to do a certain thing, or to go to a certain place, until it has been made unmistakably clear. In spite of the fact that Paul often used the expression, "if God wills," some say that such a phrase indicates lack of faith. There is a place where so-called faith becomes presumption. It is possible to confuse one's own will with that of the Lord. Saying that one is going to be healed of a disease or that one is called of God to do a certain work may be nothing more than a pitiful attempt to convince oneself.

James warned against any departure from Paul's humility and good sense in discerning God's will when he wrote, "you ought to say:

> "If the Lord will, we shall live, and do this, or that" (James 4:15).

It is not always God's will for a believer to have abounding physical health, or a large income, or long life. Those who have had some wonderful personal experience of Christ's power to heal, or to provide, or to guide are usually those who have been much in secret prayer rather than much in public proclamation about the matter.

Since God leads us step by step, without unveiling distant vistas of what lies ahead for us, we must be willing to leave our future entirely in his hands. If we knew too much of his plan, forthcoming joys and privileges might make the present seem drab and unattractive; impending troubles and sorrows would certainly make us unhappy.

Lack of knowledge of the future need not disturb us at any time, for "our sufficiency is of God" (2 Corinthians 3:5). There is a present ministry of the Holy Spirit designed to overcome our inability to select our own path, or to choose what is best.

> For we do not know what we should pray for as we ought, but the Spirit Himself makes intercession for us with groanings which cannot be uttered. Now He who searches the hearts knows what the mind of the Spirit is, because He makes intercession for the saints according to the will of God (Romans 8:26–27 NKJV).

To this provision may be added the prayers of other believers (Colossians 1:9; 4:12) and the privilege of going to the Lord ourselves for guidance (Romans 1:10).

2. The place for counsel

Vocational guidance has its place in the discovery of natural talents that may be developed or opportunities that should be seized. But no counselor has either the wisdom or the right to advise a believer in specific terms as to the work God has called him to do. Only the Lord is able perfectly to fit a personality and a lifework together.

There is always a place for sound counsel by men of God, and "he who heeds counsel is wise" (Proverbs 12:15). Pastoral advice to believers is doubtless provided for in Hebrews 13:7, 17:

> Remember them which have rule over you, who have spoken unto you the word of God: whose faith follow, considering the end of their [conduct]. . . . Obey them that have rule over you, and submit yourselves, for they watch for your souls, as they that must give account.

However, since we all have direct access to God, the New Testament is almost silent on this subject. The counsel of godly Christians is of value, but the question of what a person is to do as a lifework must be settled between the individual and God. When Paul's friends in Caesarea endeavored to keep him from going to Jerusalem, where serious trouble awaited him, he was obliged to reject their counsel; and they "ceased, saying, "'The will of the Lord be done'" (Acts 21:14).

A church may discern that the hand of God has been laid upon someone for a particular service, so that one man is granted a place of leadership and another is sent forth as a missionary, but it is the Holy Spirit who calls people to the work they are to do and moves in such a way that they are separated unto that work (Acts 13:2–3).

3. *Our cooperation is necessary*

God does not force his program on his people beyond the limits suggested in such verses as 1 Corinthians

11:31–32, which explain why the chastening of God is sometimes necessary.

> For if we would judge ourselves, we should not be judged. But when we are judged, we are chastened by the Lord, that we should not be condemned with the world.

Our cooperation with the divine program is required, "For we are God's fellow workers" (1 Corinthians 3:9 NKJV). We are admonished:

> Work out your own salvation with fear and trembling; for it is God who works in you both to will and to do for His good pleasure (Philippians 2:12–13 NKJV).

Although some have read only the first part of this portion of Scripture, and have supposed that it calls on Christians to work for their salvation, the passage plainly teaches that, since God is working within us to bring about his own will through us, we must produce outward evidences of the inward salvation which the Holy Spirit has wrought.

From the moment we receive Christ, God begins to dwell in our hearts (2 Corinthians 6:16) and to work in such a way as to make us want to do his pleasure rather than our own. We may refuse to cooperate with the indwelling Holy Spirit; but when we submit to his leading, we become living examples of the realization of the ideal set forth in Hebrews 13:21 (NKJV):

> Complete in every good work to do His will, working in you what is well pleasing in His sight, through Jesus Christ.

The surrender of all self-will is a necessary prelude to

our knowing God's program. Those who have the attitude that they will see what God's plan for them is, and then decide whether or not to adopt it, are defeating any prospect of learning the divine program. Willingness to do what God wants us to do is a basic secret of knowing his will and receiving his blessing.

Self-surrender is placed first in Romans 12:1–2. In Malachi 3:10 (NKJV), God first requires submission to his Word, and then promises:

> "Try Me now in this,"
> Says the Lord of hosts,
> "If I will not open for you the windows of heaven
> And pour out for you such blessing
> That there will not be room enough to receive it."

Christ said in Matthew 6:33 (NKJV):

> "Seek first the kingdom of God and His righteousness, and all these things shall be added to you."

The man who says, "Lord, bless my business and I will give to your work out of the proceeds," is putting the cart before the horse. We may not dictate the conditions under which we shall be willing to obey the Lord. In all things he must have the preeminence (Colossians 1:18).

4. Ample provision is made for our own initiative

Seeking and following God's plan mean the giving up of our own initiative. The person who does his lifework as unto Christ will be "not lagging in diligence, fervent in spirit, serving the Lord" (Romans 12:11). Laziness is dealt with throughout the Bible in very plain language (Proverbs 24:30–34). Energetic action appears in many phrases: "abounding in the work of the Lord" (1 Corinthians

15:58), not weary "while doing good" (Galatians 6:9); "fruitful in every good work" (Colossians 1:10); "abound more and more" (1 Thessalonians 4:1).

The empire builders of the Middle East gave way to the lethargy afterward seen in China and other eastern nations because they adopted a religion of fatalism. Believing they had no control of their fate, they refused to act on their own initiative but awaited nirvana instead. Determinism produces the same result today among those who hold they are not responsible for what they do because they are creatures of their environment.

How far above such shortsighted, pagan concepts is the Bible's teaching about divine guidance! It requires the active cooperation of every human faculty and calls forth the best that is in man by providing the incentives he needs. We know that God cares for us, plans a wonderful life for us, confirms his plan by providential circumstances, rewards us now and afterward for devoting our energies to the work he has given us to do.

Instead of idly waiting for what is sometimes called "a leading," the Spirit-filled Christian is redeeming the time, seizing every opportunity, making the most of his gifts, pressing forward, seeking new ways to carry on effectively for his Lord. In the words of Isaiah 54:2–3, he is enlarging the place of his tent, lengthening his cords, strengthening his stakes, in preparation for breaking forth on the right hand and on the left, and seeking the salvation of the lost. Every time a new movement for God has been born, it has sprung from one man or from a few individuals devoted to the doing of God's perfect will.

5. There is no limit to what we can accomplish

Probably no one has ever made the most of his possibilities. We know this is usually true in school and in our daily work, and it is also true of our Christian experience. Suppose we have hitherto missed God's plan for us. This does not mean that we are obliged now to take an inferior second- or third-best plan, for the Lord always has awaiting us his very best. It is never too late to enter into the fullness of his blessing by beginning to do what he wants us to do.

Some years ago, a drunkard was on his way to drown himself as a hopeless wreck, when he was saved by the power of Christ. It was not long before he was nationally known for the extensiveness and power of his peculiar ministry to outcasts. He founded rescue missions all over America. His case is unique. Every city has people who achieved success in various occupations because they turned themselves over to Christ. Who shall say there is a limit to what God can do through someone who has missed God's best through many years?

God is able to make a world-wide blessing of anyone who is wholly subject to him. He is

> able to do exceeding abundantly above all that we ask or think, according to the power that [works] in us (Ephesians 3:20).

The most remarkable thing about this verse is not what it says about God's ability, but what it says about the condition by which his exceedingly abundant goodness is bestowed upon us. When we allow his power to work in us, there is no limit to what he may do through us.

Present circumstances must not be permitted to discourage us. Others may have a better education, a more attractive personality, a more handsome face or figure, a stronger voice, a better memory, a keener intellect, a larger amount of time for study, more money, better clothes, more influential friends, more good books, or larger opportunities to advance in their chosen vocation. Not one of these things is of first importance, but these encouraging words are indispensable:

> I can do all things through Christ who strengthens me (Philippians 4:13 NKJV).

America is the place where farm boys may become president, and where obscure people rise to places of leadership. What is true of our nation is more wonderfully true of the kingdom of God, wherein even the giving of a cup of cold water for the sake of Christ brings a reward (Mark 9:41).

> See a man who excels in his work? He will stand before kings; He will not stand before unknown men (Proverbs 22:29 NKJV).

David among the sheep and Elisha following the plow were just as much in God's place for them as when they were later elevated to positions of honor.

Outward appearances have nothing to do with what God may have planned for us. Not often are we given a great work to do until we have proved ourselves in a small work. When we take the step just ahead, God will open the way a little farther. When we fill the place in which we find ourselves now, we thereby prove we are fit to be trusted with greater responsibilities. The faithful discharge of our present task will often become the means to an open door leading to a greater work.

6. No two believers have the same work to do

> There are diversities of gifts. . . . But one and the same

83

> Spirit works all these things, distributing to each one individually as He wills (1 Corinthians 12:4, 11 NKJV).

By the sovereign choice of the Holy Spirit, various gifts are given to us. No one has every gift, but by the faithful use of what a believer possesses, he may expect greater gifts. We are to earnestly desire the "best gifts" (1 Corinthians 12:31) and to "desire spiritual gifts" (1 Corinthians 14:1). The most unpromising people have achieved notable success because they proved themselves faithful, whether they were teachers or leaders within the church, or "helps" (1 Corinthians 12:28), that is, men and women carrying on their business or profession or daily tasks as the best way they knew to further the work of the Lord.

Since there are various gifts, some believers achieve more prominence in the world than others. There may be a great musician, a famous statesman, a noted artist, or a successful merchant in the graduating class of some school. The other graduates may face comparative mediocrity in the sight of the world. What then happens to the teaching about the God-planned life? The answer is that there is no mediocrity, no service of little value, in the sight of God. Some who are prominent now will be obscure for eternity; some who are unknown to men now will finally be highly honored (Luke 13:30).

Young believers should be careful about imitating others. It is better to be a voice than an echo. When Peter was too much concerned with what John was to do, the Lord said to him:

> "What is that to you? You follow Me" (John 21:22 NKJV).

The person who imagines he could be a greater success

if he could only step into a larger, established work, or who thinks he could do better if he occupied a position held by someone else, is revealing an unhealthy, morbid attitude. God can be trusted to give our native abilities full play, to make a place for our particular combination of talents.

> A man's gift [makes] room for him, and [brings] him before great men (Proverbs 18:16).

When we do willingly what God wants us to do, our reward is sure (1 Corinthians 9:16–17); yet we must remember the exhortation:

> You have need of endurance, so that after you have done the will of God, you may receive the promise (Hebrews 10:36 NKJV).

God is looking for those today about whom he will be able to say, as he said about David:

> I have found David the son of Jesse, a man after My own heart, who will do all My will (Acts 13:22 NKJV).

We may not be of kingly stature in this life, but God has chosen us that we should know his will (Acts 22:14), and "He who calls you is faithful, who also will do it" (1 Thessalonians 5:24 NKJV).

7. Our eternal rewards depend on present faithfulness

In the parable found in Matthew 25:14–30, Christ explained something about this matter of varying gifts, a subject that has troubled many Christians who look upon themselves as "one-talent" people. The Lord has given each of his servants talents "according to his own ability"

(v. 15 NKJV). But when we stand before him, he will reward us solely on the basis of the way we have used our gifts. The quality or size of our talents will not be the issue. A five-talent man will receive precisely the same reward as a two-talent man, if both have been equally faithful (vv. 21, 23).

Still, it is evident that some of God's children are more faithful to their trust than others. How will this be handled in the day of the judgment seat of Christ? The answer is found in the parable of Luke 19:11–27, where each servant is depicted as possessing just one pound. Whereas Matthew 25 views our varying gifts as they appear to men, Luke 19 views them as God sees them, and each man's gift is equally important.

The comparison is therefore based on what the several servants did with the work the Lord gave them to do. Luke 19:13 is, literally, "Carry on business until I come." The one who does his Lord's will most faithfully receives the highest reward. A pound becomes a city. Servants become rulers. Perfect justice is finally done. The principle is, "You were faithful over a few things, I will make you ruler over many things." We may count on the Lord's fitting our eternal reward to the degree of faithfulness to him that we have demonstrated during our life on the earth. "Shall not the Judge of all the earth do right?" (Genesis 18:25). Our success in the eyes of men may not have been very great; but when we stand before the judgment seat of Christ, it will not be our success, but our faithfulness that will be the measure of what he bestows on us as our eternal reward.

8

Discovering God's Will

Having considered the major passages of Scripture that deal with the subject of God's will, we now turn to general biblical truths about God's will. They give us some simple, comprehensive, practical rules by which any sincere Christian can discover for himself God's plan for his life.

AN IMPORTANT SCRIPTURE

The central New Testament teaching on God's will is found in Romans 12:1–2, which presents a summary of what the Lord expects of us and an appeal based on his love and mercy:

I beseech you therefore, brethren, by the mercies of
God, that you present your bodies a living sacrifice,
holy, acceptable to God, which is your reasonable
service. And do not be conformed to this world, but
be transformed by the renewing of your mind, that
you may prove what is that good and acceptable and
perfect will of God.

1. We make a choice

Notice that this is an earnest entreaty, not a command.
We can resist God's pleadings if we choose, but we shall
suffer loss now and forever if we do. He yearns for our glad
and willing service. He bases his appeal on what he has
already done for us. He urges us to present our bodies "a
living sacrifice" because of the "mercies of God," so com-
pletely described in the earlier chapters of Romans. Romans 12:1–2 is addressed to true believers who appreciate
their great salvation and will therefore respond to the call
of God.

2. Three important truths

Three distinct elements appear. As in Proverbs 3:5–6,
the first and third are positive, while the second is negative. We are to present our bodies to God, to refrain from
worldly conformity, and to be transformed. The thought-
ful student observes a striking similarity between Solomon's threefold rule and this New Testament counterpart.
Trust in God is to be entire, exclusive, and transfiguring.
It yields definite results. God will direct our path, and we
shall on our part prove how good, acceptable, and perfect
is his will for us.

"*Present your bodies a living sacrifice, holy, acceptable to
God.*" At the threshold of this passage stands an act of

dedication by which we turn our bodies over to God once for all, to be his for whatever purpose he may have for us. Christ completed his work as a dying sacrifice. He now needs living sacrifices for his present work.

Our act of dedication is to lead to a process of continuous yieldedness to the Lord, described by three terms. As *living sacrifices*, we must of necessity have renounced self-interest and self-will. As *holy*, we must confess and be forgiven of known sin. As *acceptable* to God, we must be of use to him, submitting to what his Word teaches about our life and work. It is indeed only reasonable that we should comply with his request.

"Do not be conformed to this world." There is nothing around us that can give us real peace, joy, or satisfaction apart from the Lord. Therefore, we are warned against conforming our lives to the pattern supplied by the world, when we have in Christ the pattern given by God.

"Be transformed by the renewing of your mind." The key to the meaning of "transformed" is found in the three other places in the New Testament where the same word occurs in the original Greek.

The English word *transformed* in Romans 12:2 is a translation of the same Greek word translated "transfigured" in Matthew 17:2 and Mark 9:2 to describe what happened to Christ. Look up these passages. Even now we are to live transfigured lives, as citizens of heaven in communion with the Father in glory. Second Corinthians 3:18 (where the same Greek word is used) tells how this may be achieved. We are to keep beholding Christ in the mirror of the Word, and as we do the Spirit of God will make us like him. This is not an external action produced by our keeping a set of rules, but an inward renewing by the Holy Spirit as the mind dwells on spiritual and heavenly things, rather than on things of the earth (2 Corinthians 4:18).

3. *The result of the best choice*

The sure result is that we are able to "prove what is that good, and acceptable, and perfect will of God" (Romans 12:2). We discover for ourselves God's particular plan for us, and we also demonstrate to the world around, as well as to our own satisfaction, that God's will is everything the Word of God claims for it. Instead of shrinking from his will as something to be feared, we come to recognize joyfully that everything he plans for his children is born of his love and his desire for our greatest good. We know that all things work together for our blessing, for we love him and are called according to his purpose (Romans 8:28).

FIVE PRACTICAL RULES

Most Christians who believe that God has a plan for their lives also have certain favorite portions of Scripture laid away in their hearts for their guidance. We have seen how frequently such brief summaries of truth are sprinkled throughout the Bible. It is well, however, to provide ourselves with a few brief rules that bring together the leading principles by which we may determine the will of God. Anyone can make up such a list, and a great many details could be included that do not appear here. It is in the interest of simplicity and brevity that omission is made of all reference to the necessity for the new birth, separation from sin, belief in the Bible as the Word of God, and other prerequisites of such fundamental importance that they must underlie any serious effort to learn the divine plan. Five rules will suffice.

1. There must be honest willingness to do God's will

This may seem so obvious on the face of it, so apparent from what has already been said, that it might be taken for granted; but this seems to be the chief stumbling block for most Christians. As Christ said of the city of Jerusalem that had rejected him, "You were not willing!" (Matthew 23:37). The human wills of the Jews thwarted his purpose to bless them.

By nature, we prefer our own way. This is the very essence of sin (Isaiah 53:6). Self-will keeps more people from enjoying the blessings of the God-planned life than any other factor. Many reserve the right to refuse to do what God indicates as his choice for them. They plead with God to be allowed to have what they want, instead of resting in his wisdom and love. Parents who have demanded that a dying child be restored to them have lived to regret bitterly their insistence on their own way. Young people who have married in defiance of the warning against marrying non-Christians have paid dearly for self-will.

The prophet Balaam provides us with an illustration. The princes of Moab wanted him to curse Israel. When he asked God about it, the answer was, "You shall not go with them" (Numbers 22:12). This was an explicit and plain direction, *the directive will of God*. But Balaam was not satisfied. When greater earthly honor and reward were offered him than before, he went to the Lord once more, hoping that God had changed his mind. The second reply he received is an example of *the permissive will of God*. With fine irony, God allowed the prophet to have his own way (vv. 20–22). Balaam went on from disobedience to the express revelation of God's plan for him to open sin (Numbers 31:16), and finally to death by violence, which overtook him in the midst of his anticipated enjoyment of the wages of unrighteousness (Joshua 13:22).

2. God's will is always in harmony with God's Word

If we feel a desire to do something that conflicts with the plain teaching of the Bible, we may be sure the prompting comes from the world, the flesh, or the devil. It cannot be the will of God because he cannot contradict himself. Every opportunity we face, every "leading" we think may be from the Lord, must be tested by the written Word. In this we have the example of Christ when he was tempted by Satan to act of his own volition, apart from the Father's will. He gave us the secret of victory in the words, "It is written" (Luke 4:4–8).

Certain occupations are at once excluded by the Bible as unfit for Christians. We may not take a position that would require us to bear false witness or to be dishonest. We must avoid any work that would put us in the position of ministering to the weakness or the sin of someone else. The Scriptures seek to guard us against the way of wickedness.

> Avoid it, pass not by it, turn from it, and pass away (Proverbs 4:15).

Temptation is to be avoided as much as possible (Matthew 6:13).

Where God has already given clear directions about a certain matter, he cannot be expected to make a personal revelation about it to someone who is ignorant of his Word. Stealing, murder, adultery, covetousness, and a host of other sins named in Scripture are always wrong, no matter what the circumstances. God has revealed his will about almost every conceivable problem of human conduct. Although the meaning of a scriptural passage may be obscure to us, we must never allow that fact to make us forget a plain "you shall not."

Some people use the Bible in a strange way for guidance. It is a magic oracle to some people. Instead of feeding regularly on its teachings, they open it at random, look at the first verse that meets their eye, and take it as God's message to them for the moment. There is no doubt that God has often brought a certain verse to the attention of one of his children in an unusual and almost miraculous manner for a special need, but his Word was never intended to be consulted in a superstitious manner.

Others are always "putting out a fleece"; yet there is no verse instructing us to do what Gideon did. He did this in his hour of weakness, during a terrible national crisis, when a greater responsibility rested upon him than most of us are called to bear. The "sign" of Judges 6:17 and the miracles of verses 37–40 were given to a man who had no Bible to teach him and at a time when God tested his messengers to distinguish them from false prophets.

When Zacharias, in New Testament days, asked for a sign to confirm the word of God's angel, he was stricken dumb because he did not believe (Luke 1:18–20).

In view of Christ's words, "An evil and adulterous generation seeks after a sign, and no sign" (Matthew 12:39), we must be careful that our "fleece" is not simply an evidence of unbelief or unwillingness to do what we know God wants us to do.

God in his grace has often honored the faith of those who, having exhausted every other means of knowing his will without apparent success, have asked him for some indication of what they should do, to keep them from making a serious mistake. But in the experience of great saints of God, such cases are the exception and not the rule.

In cases of doubt, a more reasonable use of the Scriptures is followed by many Christians. They set aside an evening for the reading of the Bible. They read with the earnest prayer that God will speak to their hearts from his Book and suit some part of it to the immediate need.

Thus one believer, faced with two possible courses to pursue, both equally desirable and in keeping with God's previously revealed plan, began reading in the Psalms, seeking light from the Lord. At length his heart was warmed by one verse that fit the situation. He made that verse his prayer, believing God had spoken through it in answer to his earlier petitions. He prayed:

> Cause me to hear Your lovingkindness in the
> morning,
> For in You do I trust;
> Cause me to know the way in which I should walk,
> For I lift up my soul to You (Psalm 143:8 NKJV).

He was awakened the next day by the ringing of the telephone, and the message was of such a nature that his choice was easy.

3. Providential circumstances may indicate God's will

When our present circumstances are directly opposed to what we think is the Lord's will for us, we must be careful lest we be insisting on our own way rather than his. He is the God of circumstance. He can and will change every factor in a given situation if he wants us somewhere else than where we are.

Sometimes the romance of the mission field has made young people feel "a call" to go to a far country, but they never were able to go, try as they might. Since it is impossible for God to call someone to do a work for him without providing for every need and removing every obstacle, the young people simply misunderstood the will of God.

> Let each one remain in the same calling in which he was called (1 Corinthians 7:20 NKJV).

One young man, after an unusual experience at the time of his conversion, felt that God wanted him to enter a school in a distant city to study for a certain profession. He was so sure of this that he went. Everything seemed to favor this action, except the circumstances of his home life. It was not long before a verse of Scripture, previously overlooked, made him return home again, to wait upon God for a less hasty "leading." The verse was 1 Timothy 5:8:

> But if any provide not for his own, and specially for those of his house, he [has] denied the faith, and is worse than an infidel.

When the providence of God led Joseph into Egypt as a slave, he made the best of the situation by faithfully serving God in the work at hand. Moses may have longed to be with his people Israel during the years he was a shepherd in the desert, but he waited until God intervened to bring about a change in his circumstances. It is quite possible that Dorcas may have preferred a less obscure place in the early church than as a maker of garments (Acts 9:39), but she carried on faithfully for the Lord where she was; and she was raised from the dead to continue her work, while James the apostle was not (Acts 12:2).

It seems clear that providential events must have been linked with the heavenly vision that made Paul and his friends assuredly gather that God wanted them to enter Europe instead of Asia and Bithynia (Acts 16:10). Sometimes the apostle found that circumstances demanded that he work at his trade as a tentmaker (Acts 18:3), even though "the Lord has commanded that those who preach the gospel should live from the gospel" (1 Corinthians 9:14). He wrote:

> I have learned in whatever state I am, to be content: I know how to be abased, and I know how to abound. Everywhere and in all things I have learned both to be full and to be hungry, both to abound and to suffer need (Philippians 4:11–12 NKJV).

Our present position is the place where we must begin to fulfill God's plan. A new environment will not change us into faithful servants of the Lord if we are not faithful where we are. Christ said:

> You shall be witnesses to Me in Jerusalem, and in all Judea and Samaria, and to the end of the earth (Acts 1:8 NKJV).

If we do not begin at home, at our Jerusalem, we cannot expect the Lord to enlarge our horizon; nor should we think his will for us will involve a sudden miraculous change in the circumstances where his providence has already placed us. Let us rest in the Lord where we are and wait patiently for him. He eventually will exalt us.

4. God's will is made known in answer to prayer

After his conversion on the Damascus Road, Paul

> said: "Lord, what do You want me to do?" Then the Lord said to him: "Arise and go into the city, and you will be told what you must do" (Acts 9:6 NKJV).

The desire that we find in our own hearts to know God's plan is but a faint reflection of the desire that is in the heart of God. His Word teaches us to pray:

> For You are my rock and my fortress;
> Therefore, for Your name's sake,
> Lead me and guide me (Psalm 31:3 NKJV).

> Make Your way straight before my face (Psalm 5:8 NKJV).

> Teach me Your way, O LORD;
> I will walk in Your truth (Psalm 86:11 NKJV).

Those who are most often in communion with the Lord are likely to be least often troubled about his will. When we begin the day with a period of Bible reading and prayer, we are made sensitive to his leading during the hours that follow. As we face important decisions, we find it easy to lift our hearts to him for help. We should never step out on ground over which we have not first prayed. God's Word offers us wisdom as we need it (James 1:5). We are likely to make a serious mistake if we seize some opportunity we think is God-given, without earnest prayer.

5. *Peace of mind should attend the doing of God's will*

It is evident that the divine program will be in accordance with the convictions of our highest judgment, as illuminated by the Holy Spirit. Ordinarily, there should be nothing to disturb our assurance that we are in God's will. We are promised "the peace of God, which surpasses all understanding" (Philippians 4:7 NKJV).

> Great peace have those who love Your law,
> And nothing causes them to stumble
> (Psalm 119:165 NKJV).

If this peace is absent, there is something wrong, and we had better go again to the Word of God and to prayer, or reexamine the circumstances.

Every means we have used to learn the mind of the Lord should be in agreement with every other means. He cannot deny himself; and therefore the teaching of Scripture, the answers to our prayers, the providential position in which we find ourselves, and our own intelligent convictions should all be in harmony.

This consent of the mind to the leading of the Lord, this recognition that his will is good, acceptable, and perfect, by which peace concerning the future comes to us, is a ministry of "the spirit of wisdom," who enlightens the eyes of our understanding (Ephesians 1:17–18). Sometimes people speak of "spiritual intuition," "spiritual intelligence," or an "inner light." Since many evil spirits deceive the unwary, we must always keep this inner persuasion of God's will in its proper place of subjection to the appointed means of learning his will.

> Beloved, do not believe every spirit, but test the spirits, whether they are of God (1 John 4:1 NKJV).

As we walk close to the Lord, his Word tells us:

> The anointing which you have received from Him abides in you, and you do not need that anyone teach you (1 John 2:27 NKJV).

> If [anyone] wants to do his will, he shall know of the doctrine, whether it is of God or whether I speak of myself (John 7:17).

A HELPFUL SUMMARY

Probably no better brief statement about how to discover the will of God has ever been written than that by which George Müller, one of the outstanding Christian leaders of the last century, guided his own life for Christ.

1. I seek at the beginning to get my heart into such a state that it has no will of its own in regard to a given matter. Nine-tenths of the trouble with people is just here. Nine-tenths of the difficulties are overcome when our hearts are ready to do the Lord's will, whatever it may be. When one is truly in this state, it is usually but a little way to the knowledge of what his will is.

2. Having done this, I do not leave the result to feeling or simple impression. If I do so, I make myself liable to great delusions.

3. I see the will of the Spirit of God through, or in connection with, the Word of God. The Spirit and the Word must be combined. If I look to the Spirit alone without the Word, I lay myself open to great delusions

also. If the Holy Spirit guides us at all, he will do it according to the Scriptures and never contrary to them.

4. Next I take into account providential circumstances. These often plainly indicate God's will in connection with his Word and Spirit.

5. I ask God in prayer to reveal his will to me.

6. Thus, through prayer to God, the study of the Word, and reflection, I come to a deliberate judgment according to the best of my ability and knowledge; and if my mind is thus at peace, and continues so after two or three more petitions, I proceed accordingly. In trivial matters, and in transactions involving most important issues, I have found this method always effective.

9

Difficult Questions

One of the most popular features of Bible conferences for new Christians and young people is the question-and-answer period. The fact that the same practical problems of the Christian life come up for discussion repeatedly, in various parts of the country, is an indication that there is a widespread need for a frank statement about them, in the light of the Scriptures and the available facts.

When people inquire about these matters that puzzle them, they expect a straightforward answer. Which amusements are right for believers? Which are wrong, and just why are they wrong? What about friendships with unbelievers? Can a Protestant boy expect happiness if he marries a Catholic girl? Should Christians attend jazz or rock music concerts? What is the harm in cards, in smoking, in dancing, in lotteries? How about the movies, the theater, the opera? Is there any reason why a Christian boy or girl should not dress like their schoolmates?

These are typical questions. Those who ask them have every right to a clear and unequivocal answer from their spiritual leaders. Unfortunately, they do not always receive it. There is sometimes a division of opinion among speakers at a conference. Uncertainty and spiritual unrest are the inevitable result. If the leaders disagree, how can those who look to them for help be expected to discern the truth?

Such disagreements can easily be avoided by keeping personal prejudice out of a discussion, either for or against the point at issue. Whether a given teacher likes or dislikes a particular amusement, whether or not he thinks it right or wrong, should not be made the basis of his answer. There are definite principles of action set forth in the Word of God, and there are facts about most problems that may be ascertained. These are the two elements necessary to a satisfying answer to any question. Personal opinions that ignore the Bible or the facts of the case can only bring confusion. Expressing such opinions is scarcely being fair to the eager minds of young Christians.

THE BIBLE HAS THE ANSWER

The answer to every difficulty ever faced by the human heart is to be found in the Scripture. When a problem is faced honestly, with perfect willingness to obey the Word, there is usually no question about the solution.

> If any of you lacks wisdom, let him ask of God . . . and it shall be given him (James 1:5).

If we really want to know whether something is pleasing to the Lord, he will not permit us to remain long in the dark about it. Ordinarily, the trouble is not lack of teaching in the Bible, but unwillingness to follow what it does teach. The key to knowing the mind of Christ is readiness to do his will when it is revealed.

The great principles stated in the New Testament to govern us in doubtful matters are best understood in the light of the early history of the church. In apostolic days, the church was faced with problems just as we are today. In the wisdom of God, they were solved in such a way as to provide guideposts for believers during all the changing centuries to follow.

1. Problems of sin

Some problems had to do with matters that were plainly sin. These were dealt with in no uncertain fashion. Believers were forbidden to take each other to court (1 Corinthians 6:1–8). Those guilty of sins against the body were condemned (1 Corinthians 5). Obedience to government was enjoined (Romans 13:1–7). Many such clear commands are to be found.

2. Problems of personal choice

There were other problems, however, which did not involve clearcut moral and ethical issues. They dealt rather with matters of personal choice, where no written law of God applied, now that Christ had become "the end of the law for righteousness to everyone who believes" (Romans 10:4).

Instead of a "you shall not" in these cases where godly men might differ, the Holy Spirit was pleased to enunciate principles for the guidance of believers ever afterward. The two difficulties that gave rise to these fundamental rules had to do with the eating of meats that had been offered for sacrifice in idol temples, and with the observing of certain days as holier than others.

In great cities like Rome and Corinth, meat dealers secured their supplies partly from pagan temples where the animals had been offered in sacrifice. One could not always tell whether a purchase came from this source or from another. Nor did anyone care very much until the Gospel came and Christians began to face the question of how they should conduct themselves in pagan surroundings.

Should believers use meat that might have come from an idol temple? There was a division of opinion. One group refused to eat meat of any kind. Even though it might not have been dedicated to some pagan god, it was likely to be ceremonially unclean as judged by the law of Moses. The other group held that it was perfectly proper for them to eat what they pleased. A pagan ceremony could not affect the essential qualities of the food they found offered for sale, and is not every creature of God good (1 Timothy 4:3–5)?

The second subject of controversy concerned the keeping of special days. Christians with a Jewish background liked to observe the holy days of ancient Israel. The Jewish Sabbath was a convenient time for worship. Others preferred to follow the example of the apostles by meeting on the Lord's Day (Luke 24:33–36; Acts 20:7). Still others regarded every day as holy unto the Lord (Romans 14:5), and they tried to make every day the same in the life they lived for him.

THREE GUIDING PRINCIPLES IN PROBLEMS OF CHOICE

Both of these problems of choice were dealt with in

such a way as to make it possible for the church to solve every point of dispute in the future. Instead of treating the two questions as temporary difficulties that would lose their significance with the passing of time, the Holy Spirit devoted three long passages of the New Testament to them, making them the basis of principles to be followed throughout the entire Church Age. The extended discussion of these sample problems is found in Romans 14; 1 Corinthians 8; 10:23–33.

1. Personal liberty in Christ

The proper attitude of Christians toward those who differed with them was enunciated in Romans 14:1–4. The man who restricted his diet to vegetables was forbidden to sit in judgment on his brother who ate whatever he wanted. On the other hand, the man who was convinced that there was no wrong in eating doubtful meats was told not to despise his brother who refused them.

The bearing of this passage of Scripture on the believer's problems today is of great importance. No one has the right to stand on a platform and say, "You are sinning if you do the thing I consider wrong," when the Bible has not ruled on the matter. Neither has anyone the right to accuse someone else of narrowness or bigotry because that person conscientiously refrains from something in which others see no harm. Nor is there justification here for thinking ourselves to be strong in the faith just because we have no compunctions about indulging in a questionable pleasure, for it may contain elements that mark it as contrary to the spirit of Christ.

To abstain from fleshly lusts requires a stronger faith than to indulge them. A Christian who remains aloof from a doubtful practice just because he wants to please

Christ is giving evidence of spiritual health far beyond that of the self-indulgent man who has never given up anything for the Lord's sake.

There is abundant testimony in the Bible to the fact that *we have freedom of action as children of God, within the limits he has set.* The law as a "yoke of bondage" has been lifted from us (Galatians 5:1). Once Israel was given laws about meats. Now "food does not commend us to God; for neither if we eat are we the better, nor if we do not eat are we the worse" (1 Corinthians 8:8).

Once there were laws given about holy days. Now, "one person esteems one day above another; another esteems every day alike. Let each be fully convinced in his own mind" (Romans 14:5). It is evident that, in cases where there is no moral issue involved, God has placed Christian conduct on a different basis from that of Israel in Old Testament times. We now have freedom to serve the Lord in accordance with the dictates of our own conscience, subject only to his Word and his Spirit (Galatians 5:16, 18).

This first principle lifts the spirit of bondage from the believer (Romans 8:15). Considered apart from other higher principles of action, it helps to solve some problems that have perplexed Christians, such as the Sunday question. There are people whose only means of livelihood involves work on Sunday because they are connected, let us say, with an industry that provides light, heat, water, or transportation to an entire community, including churches and hospitals. Are they sinning against God, and are others sinning who use the public services that make Sunday employment necessary? The principle of Christian liberty makes it clear that this is not at all a question of breaking the law of God, and the burden is gone from many a conscience.

We gather for worship on Sunday by common consent, and not because the law of the Lord requires that particular day. God has always honored such gatherings, ever since the Lord Jesus was present at the first one (Luke 24:36), but he has also honored the testimony of individuals who were unable to be present for reasons they could conscientiously give to him. There is a basic human need for which God made provision by giving Israel the Sabbath at Sinai (Nehemiah 9:13–14). We want to do all we can to keep the Lord's Day holy unto him, out of love for him; but we know that he understands if we must work on that day.

> Let no one judge you in food or in drink, or regarding a festival or . . . sabbaths (Colossians 2:16 NKJV).

Likewise, we are not sinning against the law of Christ if we partake of foods once forbidden to Israel. There are important sanitary reasons, since discovered by scientists, which explain why God did not permit his people to eat the flesh of scavengers, carnivorous animals, and other "unclean beasts." It is profitable to know the ancient regulations governing clean and unclean animals, but the Christian who eats ham, for example, is not a lawbreaker.

> There is nothing unclean of itself; but to him who considers anything to be unclean, to him it is unclean (Romans 14:14 NKJV).

There are definite limits to this first principle of action set forth in the Bible. The liberty wherewith Christ made us free is not liberty to sin.

> Shall we sin, because we are not under the law, but under grace? God forbid! (Romans 6:15).

107

Those who practice sin have simply never been born again.

> Whoever has been born of God does not sin, for His seed remains in him; and he cannot sin, because he has been born of God (1 John 3:9 NKJV).

Repeatedly, the Holy Spirit warns us against misunderstanding or twisting the blessed teaching about liberty in Christ in such a way as to result in harm. "You, brethren, have been called to liberty; only do not use liberty as an opportunity for the flesh, but through love serve one another" (Galatians 5:13). We are free so that we may voluntarily become servants of Christ (1 Corinthians 7:22).

Because we have liberty in Christ, we are not free to neglect the Bible, prayer, Christian witness, the fellowship of other Christians, our responsibilities to the church, to our fellow men, or to God. We are not free to do anything that injures our bodies, which are the temples of the Holy Spirit (1 Corinthians 6:19–20). We are to "seek those things which are above, where Christ is, sitting at the right hand of God" (Colossians 3:1), to walk worthy of the calling wherewith we are called (Ephesians 4:1), and to be faithful in everything that is part of our duty and privilege as believers.

2. Our neighbor's good

This is a higher motive for action than personal liberty.

> All things are lawful, but not all things are profitable. All things are lawful, but not all things edify. Let no one seek his own good, but that of his neighbor (1 Corinthians 10:23–24 NASB).

That which might be perfectly all right for us, if we judged it by its effect on our own spiritual lives, might be very wrong when judged by its effect on a weaker Christian.

> Beware lest somehow this liberty of yours become a stumbling block to those who are weak (1 Corinthians 8:9 NKJV).

Here is a man, let us say, who likes to see horses running. It is lawful for him to do so. If he attended a horse race, his own spiritual life might not be harmed. But he has a friend or neighbor who has a weakness for gambling. This friend is led by his example to go to the races. The effect of seeing people place their wagers is strong enough to awaken in this second man a passion to win a little easy money. He is soon plunged into soul-destroying sin, which ruins not only the man himself but his family as well. The Christian responsible has paid a terrible price for pleasing himself.

A more common illustration is to be seen in the Christian who "takes a drink." Medical science has discovered that a certain percentage of all drinkers become drunkards. No one can tell which man or woman has this weakness. Through the influence of a man who is able to drink with moderation, another man is led to take his first glass of liquor. This second individual finds that a sleeping demon has been awakened. He becomes an alcoholic, a pitiable creature of the saloons and the gutter.

> Do not destroy with your food the one for whom Christ died (Romans 14:15 NKJV).

We may put any questionable amusement, habit, or practice in place of the word *food* in this or the parallel verses stating the same great principle. When others are hurt by our self-indulgence, we are not walking in love. When we embolden the conscience of a weak brother by something we do that does not seem to hurt us, so that he is ruined, we sin against our brother, and therefore we sin against Christ, even though no law has been written about a particular indulgence (1 Corinthians 8:10–12).

Many believers' problems would be solved if they adopted this rule. Anything is wrong that might lead someone else astray. If it could keep an unsaved man or woman from seriously considering the salvation we profess, then let us avoid it for their sakes, no matter how harmless it might otherwise be.

In writing to the churches of Corinth and Rome, the apostle Paul, by inspiration, stated this principle emphatically as his own rule of life:

> If food makes my brother stumble, I will never again eat meat, lest I make my brother stumble (1 Corinthians 8:13 NKJV).

> It is good neither to eat meat nor drink wine nor do anything by which your brother stumbles or is offended or is made weak (Romans 14:21 NKJV).

It was because of this principle that the Lord Jesus performed the miracle of the tribute money. He, the Creator and Sustainer of the universe, might have been considered above the necessity of paying taxes to the Roman government; but he sent Peter for the money and gave as the reason, "lest we offend them" (Matthew 17:27). We too must "have regard for good things in the sight of all men" (Romans 12:17 NKJV). We must "abstain from every form of evil" (1 Thessalonians 5:22 NKJV).

3. *The glory of God*

Whether you eat or drink, or whatever you do, do all
to the glory of God (1 Corinthians 10:31 NKJV).

This is the highest motive one can possibly follow: to
do everything so that honor and praise may be given to
God. How we may seek to conform our actions to this
ideal is suggested in a related series of exhortations in
Colossians 3:17, 23 (NKJV):

And whatever you do in word or deed, do all in the
name of the Lord Jesus, giving thanks to God the
Father through Him. . . . And whatever you do, do it
heartily, as to the Lord and not to men.

Here are some distinct tests that may be applied to a
given act: Can it be done in the name of the Lord Jesus?
That is, can we do it as those who bear his name before
others, bringing praise and honor to his name instead of
reproach? Can we perform the action thankfully, expressing gratitude to God for the privilege, and asking his
blessing upon it in prayer? Is it possible for us to do it
heartily as unto the Lord, which means for his sake, and
as though he were present?

This principle applies to actions that could have little
or no effect on our neighbors. For example, we are free to
use our spare time as we please, within certain limits. If
we find ourselves alone, shall we read a questionable
magazine or a profitable book? Shall we play solitaire or
study the Scriptures? Shall we do our homework or watch
television? If we have in view the glory of God, it will make
a difference in our choice. What will be the most likely to
produce in us that which will enable us better to represent
him as his ambassadors? If we are weary, either rest or

relaxation is doubtless the answer. If our work at school is a discredit to the Lord we love, we had better study. If we have been too much indoors, a walk or a bicycle ride may be the best thing we could do for God's glory.

Let us apply this third principle to the subject of sports. It is evident that we have personal liberty to engage in any beneficial recreation. Likewise, there is no honest basis for refusing to play a clean game, or to watch such a game, lest some weak brother be led astray. What about the third rule for action? Can we play tennis or baseball, or shoot at a target, to the glory of God? Most certainly we can!

The Lord knows our frame. He has made us so that physical and mental exercises are necessary to our well-being, when indulged in temperately. All work and no play make Jack a dull boy. If our recreation is such that it can be enjoyed without bringing any discredit on the name of the Lord, with thanksgiving for the privilege, and heartily as unto him, we may be sure we are doing no wrong to enter wholeheartedly into the fun. On the other hand, if it is something we would not want to do if he were present, because we know it might harm us morally, physically, or spiritually, we had better leave it alone.

Let us suppose that a game becomes an obsession. We would rather play basketball than eat. We begin to neglect other things. Our grades at school are not good. We no longer find time for Bible study and Christian fellowship and service. Or perhaps we are spending more money than we should on records or tapes. Or we have taken up something that begins to injure our health, or threatens to keep us from giving an honest day's work for an honest day's pay.

What then? We still have liberty in Christ. We still may feel that we are not a stumbling block before others;

our influence is not hurting anyone else. But anything that adversely affects our spiritual life, undermines our health, or tends to hurt our testimony before the world is not something that can be said to glorify God. We love him; we are sincere in our desire to serve the One who has saved us. Therefore, we must restore the balance to our lives by putting recreation back where it belongs. We must put first things first and, even though it may seem like a great sacrifice, give up anything that interferes with our accomplishing the high purpose for which the Lord has placed us on the earth, "that we . . . should be to the praise of His glory" (Ephesians 1:12).

10

What Does God Expect of Us?

No matter what may be the daily work to which God has called us or what gifts we possess or what our interests and our circumstances may be or how much time is at our disposal or how great the responsibilities resting on our shoulders, there is a divine standard of Christian life and service to which we must conform if we want to be faithful ambassadors of Christ in the world. The fact that the pastor of the church we attend is devoting all of his time to the work of God does not change our own status as representatives of our absent Lord or affect our personal obligations to God.

Even though we may lead the singing at a worship

service or use our talents to plan a rally or give large sums of money to the mission field or serve on an important committee or teach a Sunday school class or do any other thing to advance the cause of Christ, we still face the revealed truth that God expects a certain kind of life from us as believers. This life is not dependent upon the fact that we are doing a special work for him; nor is it basically influenced or altered in any way by the vocation we follow.

What does the Lord require of us, specifically, as we live and work and play in the place to which his providence has brought us? It is not difficult to find the answer in his Word. There are passages in the Bible that state in simple language the basic rules governing the acts and attitudes of all believers.

Let us suppose we are considering a mixed group of Christians—a schoolboy, a housewife, a minister, a store-keeper, a student nurse, an electrician, a doctor, a mechanic, a teacher, a farmer, a miner, a soldier—in fact, a group as diverse as we can imagine. What are the things God expects of them all, in spite of what they do as their daily occupations and limited only by their opportunities and their varying abilities?

It would be possible to go through the Bible and make a list of hundreds of verses mentioning some aspect of the Christian life. For example, Romans 12 contains nearly forty exhortations to the people of God. However, needful as every word of Scripture is for our instruction and guidance, it is too much to expect even Christians to memorize all these precepts and then keep them all in mind every minute of every day. If we read the Bible daily, we shall remind ourselves of such details as we need in order to grow in the faith, and every small admonition will doubtless be useful to us at some time.

A SUMMARY OF WHAT GOD EXPECTS OF US

God has included in the Scriptures several summaries of truth. One of these is found in Titus 2:11–14, which may be considered as an apostles' creed, touching most of the fundamental revelations about how we are to conduct ourselves as Christians. The great Apostles' Creed which we repeat in our churches is based on the Bible, of course; but it is not in itself inspired, and it deals with what we believe rather than what God wants us to do. Anyone can memorize the inspired creed of Titus 2:11–14. Then he has at his instant command an outline of truth into which most of the specific teachings of the New Testament may be fitted as they are learned.

> For the grace of God that brings salvation has appeared to all men, teaching us that, denying ungodliness and worldly lusts, we should live soberly, righteously, and godly in the present age, looking for the blessed hope and glorious appearing of our great God and Savior Jesus Christ, who gave Himself for us, that He might redeem us from every lawless deed and purify for Himself His own special people, zealous for good works (Titus 2:11–14 NKJV).

1. The beginning of the Christian life

A remarkably concise statement of the basis of our salvation appears in verse 11, which is rendered somewhat differently in the American Standard Version:

> For the grace of God [has] appeared, bringing salvation to all men.

Three important details stand out from this text:

a. *Salvation is by grace, that is, by the unmerited favor of God.* By nature we are sinners, deserving to be judged and condemned, to be forever barred from heaven. God in mercy has lifted us from the place of judgment; God in grace has bestowed eternal life on us. The Greek word for *grace* really includes both of these aspects of salvation. Human merit is absolutely excluded. We are saved from condemnation and receive life in God's presence entirely apart from any goodness of our own.

> For by grace you have been saved through faith, and that not of yourselves; it is the gift of God, not of works, lest anyone should boast (Ephesians 2:8–9 NKJV).

Our personal faith lays hold of what God offers through grace, but this is not something for which we may take any credit; it is not of ourselves. Salvation is the free gift of God; it has nothing to do with works we may have done. Otherwise, there would be occasion for boasting on our part, as though we had contributed something toward the purchase of a ticket to heaven. Men often do boast of some religious custom, or of their personal righteousness; but they do so in defiance of the explicit Word of God.

> Where is boasting then? It is excluded
> (Romans 3:27).

b. *The grace of God has "appeared."* Literally translated, "appeared" means "has been caused to shine from above." God's grace was revealed in a Person, the Lord Jesus Christ. Of no one else was it ever written:

> The Dayspring from on high has visited us;
> To give light to those who sit in darkness

and the shadow of death,
To guide our feet into the way of peace
(Luke 1:78–79 NKJV).

No one else ever had the right to say, "I am the light of the world" (John 9:5). Into the spiritual and moral darkness of the world "the true Light" (John 1:9) came. Men beheld his glory, full of grace and truth (v. 14), and in beholding him by faith they were saved from their sins (v. 29).

c. *This salvation has been made available to all men.* No one is excluded from the offer; "whosoever will" believe in Christ is redeemed by faith in him. Whenever anyone is saved, it is always by grace.

We are not to understand that all men are given salvation, but that salvation has been brought to all men for their acceptance or rejection. You can bring a horse to water, but you cannot make him drink. God has brought salvation to men, but he does not force it on us. We were given freedom of choice by creation. Sometimes we read of men who refuse food until they die. It is also possible to refuse God's offer of eternal life through Christ; and many do, in spite of what it cost the Lord to make it available, and in spite of what it costs men to reject it. To refuse it is to experience lifelong absence of peace and joy, as well as judgment after death.

2. The negative side of the Christian life

Whereas Titus 2:11 speaks of "all men," verse 12 is confined to "us," which means believers, who are set apart from all men by the grace of God through Christ. God's grace is said to be "teaching us that, denying ungodliness and worldly lusts," we should live "soberly, righteously, and godly" (v. 12).

This is a common distinction of the Scriptures.

> He who believes in the Son has everlasting life; and
> he who does not believe the Son shall not see life, but
> the wrath of God abides on him (John 3:36 NKJV).

When Jesus said, "I am the light of the world"—a statement encompassing all of mankind—he gave a further revelation about a special light for the smaller number who trust him:

> He who follows Me shall not walk in darkness, but
> have the light of life (John 8:12 NKJV).

The grace of God *offers* salvation to all men; the grace of God *teaches* only those who accept the offer. Literally, this is "disciplining us," an expression covering every means God may use to separate us from sin.

The first part of the gracious ministry that seeks to make us walk worthy of our high calling is a negative one. We are to practice self-discipline. We must assume once for all an attitude of denial to every form of ungodliness and worldly lust.

Ungodliness is lack of reverence for God and his Word. It is not open wickedness so much as the absence of real godliness. It is the lack of that high and holy respect for God that the prophets called "the fear of the Lord." By this they meant reverential awe, the recognition of the gulf lying between the holiness of God and the sinfulness of men, a gulf so vast that it could be bridged only by the sacrifice of the Son of God. Anything that makes us lose sight of the majesty of the Lord God Almighty—whether it be a flippant presumption, a tolerant view of sin, or a careless neglect of "things that pertain unto life and godliness" (2 Peter 1:3)—is ungodliness and must be denied.

Worldly lusts are "the things in the world . . . the lust of the flesh, the lust of the eyes, and the pride of life," which men love rather than God (1 John 2:15–16). The proper Christian attitude toward these things is one of denial and aversion. This passage contemplates, not the world of good things provided by God for his people, but the world system, which is opposed to a godly life. Our fleshly natures lust after forbidden, injurious things; our eyes behold and covet that which is not ours. We tend toward pride of race, pride of face, pride of place, pride of intellect, pride of possessions, and much more.

The Christian who has never denied himself anything for Christ's sake has not made much of a beginning in the Christian life. There are many things the world loves and does that are not becoming for those who are determined to walk with God. We must refuse them our consent, tear them from our hearts by the roots, and deny them any place in our lives.

3. The positive side of the Christian life

We should live soberly, righteously, and godly, in this present age, looking for that blessed hope (Titus 2:12–13).

The larger side of the life in Christ is not negative but positive. It views our relationship in four aspects, which, taken together, present a remarkably complete picture of what God expects of us.

a. *The inward look.* "We should live soberly," or with self-restraint. There is within us, that is, within our flesh, no good thing (Romans 7:18). Desires of all kinds clamor for gratification. Even a tiny tot will rebel against his parents and seek to protect himself with untruths, until disciplined. Throughout life self-control is necessary. Since we lack the power to achieve this perfectly by ourselves, it is made one element in the fruit of the Spirit (Galatians 5:22–23). In dependence on him, we are able to live the life of constant victory.

b. *The outward look.* "We should live . . . righteously" before others. We cannot go apart from the world and live in seclusion if we would be faithful to Christ who has called us to be his witnesses to men. Since we are always surrounded by the people of the world, every word and every act of ours are bound to have an effect on others. The gospel we stand for, the Lord we love, and the testimony we bear are all discredited in the eyes of men to the degree that we fail to heed this precept of the Scriptures.

> Beware lest somehow this liberty of yours become a stumbling block to those who are weak (1 Corinthians 8:9 NKJV).

> Walk in wisdom toward those who are outside, redeeming the time. Let your speech always be with grace, seasoned with salt, that you may know how you ought to answer each one (Colossians 4:5–6 NKJV).

c. *The upward look.* "We should live . . . godly—not merely amiably and justly . . . but something higher, with reverential love toward God" (Fausset). The knowledge that "the eyes of the Lord are in every place, beholding the evil and the good" (Proverbs 15:3) adds meaning to the command:

> And whatever you do, do it heartily, as to the Lord and not to men (Colossians 3:23 NKJV).

Every moment should be lived as though we were visibly in the presence of the Lord, since "all things are naked and open to the eyes of Him to whom we must give account" (Hebrews 4:13). It is obvious that such a command as this touches on thoughts and actions about which no one except the Lord could know. It reaches into the most secret places of our hearts.

d. The forward look. "We should live . . . looking for that blessed hope." If the other three parts of this outline of the Christian life should not seem to require an aggressive witness for the Lord, this fourth one does. Every passage of Scripture describing the Second Coming of Christ should have the effect of stirring us up to active service for him.

If we are ashamed of him and his words, so that we hide our relationship to him from others, he will be ashamed of us at his coming (Luke 9:26). A crown of righteousness awaits all who love his appearing (2 Timothy 4:8). There will be weeping and gnashing of teeth on the part of those who did not receive him before the door was closed on the offer of free salvation (Luke 13:28). Although some believers will be ashamed before him at his coming (1 John 2:28), "everyone who has this hope in Him purifies himself" (3:3).

These are incentives enough to make us strive to win the lost to Christ and to live pure lives in view of the imminent return of the Lord to reward his people and the inevitable judgment that awaits the ungodly. If we are always looking for that blessed hope, we shall never go anywhere or do anything unless we are willing to have him come and find us in that place or doing that thing.

The last thought the apostle leaves with us in his summary of what God expects from believers is a reminder of the "glorious appearing of the great God and our [Savior] Jesus Christ" (Titus 2:13). We have failed to see its real importance if it has become to us more of a doctrinal hobby than a powerful stimulus to soul-winning. Those who are looking for Christ's reappearance have every reason to be zealous in proclaiming the good news of his death for sinners.

A PRACTICAL CONCLUSION

As Paul concludes his apostolic creed, he says:

> These things speak, and exhort, and rebuke with all
> authority (Titus 2:15).

What things? That God's grace has offered salvation to all men; that we should live soberly, righteously, godly, and in expectation of the Lord, and that all of these issue from the cross. Thus the cross, with which this creed begins, is the theme emphasized once more at its close. Christ "gave Himself for us, that He might redeem us from every lawless deed and purify for Himself His own special people, zealous for good works" (v.14 NKJV).

We are the people of God. We became so because we received Christ who died in our place on Calvary. He thus gave himself in order to redeem us. Peter, in writing to Christians in the early church, spoke of this as a matter of common knowledge, about which there could be no uncertainty.

You were not redeemed with corruptible things . . .
but with the precious blood of Christ, as of a lamb
without blemish and without spot (1 Peter 1:18–19
NKJV).

Entirely apart from the eternal purpose the Lord Jesus
has in store for his own, what practical purpose for this
present life did he have in mind for those whom he was
redeeming? If we want to fulfill the destiny he intended
for us when he gave himself in our stead, we shall accept
at his hand deliverance "from all iniquity," or lawlessness,
and allow him to purify us even as he is pure. We shall
recognize that we are indeed "a special people," which
means a people acquired by God for his own possession.
And finally, we shall be "zealous for good works," exhib-
iting Spirit-given zeal to live and act in such a way as to
bring glory and praise and honor to the name of the Lord
whom we serve. If we do this, the people around us will,
by our "good works which they observe, glorify God in
the day of visitation" (1 Peter 2:12).

11

A Summary of the Christian Life

If we are to have a working knowledge of what the Lord expects from us as his followers, even before we have gained that wide knowledge of the Bible that comes only from years of reading and study, we need to consider the wonderful summary of the Christian life found in Hebrews 10:19–25 (NKJV). It deals with our relationship to God, to the world, and to the church; and it embodies the three outstanding graces—faith, hope, and love.

> Therefore, brethren, having boldness to enter the Holiest by the blood of Jesus, by a new and living way which He consecrated for us, through the veil, that is, His flesh, and having a High Priest over the house

of God, let us draw near with a true heart in full assurance of faith, having our hearts sprinkled from an evil conscience and our bodies washed with pure water. Let us hold fast the confession of our hope without wavering, for He who promised is faithful. And let us consider one another in order to stir up love and good works, not forsaking the assembling of ourselves together, as is the manner of some, but exhorting one another, and so much the more as you see the Day approaching.

THE CHRISTIAN LIFE IS A LIFE OF PRAYER

Half of this passage is devoted to prayer, and prayer is put first. Scores of excellent books have been written about this most important element of any life that seeks to be well pleasing and useful to God. Prayer is the secret of power. Robert Murray McCheyne, the beauty of whose devotional life still inspires believers,[1] once wrote to a pastor who was discouraged because his preaching was not bringing the anticipated results. And this is what he wrote: "If preaching has failed, try praying." The men and women who have made the greatest spiritual impact on their generation have been men and women of prayer. The sweeping revival of 1858 followed the most remarkable prayer movement in American history.

1. The basis of prayer is "the blood of Jesus" (Hebrews 10:19)

Hebrews 10:19 tells us that "the blood of Jesus" is the

---

1 Andrew Bonar, *Memoir and Remains of Robert Murray McCheyne* (Grand Rapids: Baker Book House, 1978).

basis of prayer. Because of it, we have boldness to enter into the Holiest, that is, the presence of God. The Tabernacle of ancient Israel was a pattern of heavenly things (Hebrews 8:5). Behind the inner veil was a little room where God revealed his presence among his people. Into this Holy of Holies no one but the high priest could enter, and he only once each year, on the Day of Atonement, bearing the blood of a sacrifice offered for his own sins and the sins of the people (Hebrews 9:7–8). So terrifying was this privilege that the high priest never entered this Most Holy Place with boldness, for fire from before the Lord consumed all who dared to approach him without due regard for the provisions of his law (Numbers 16:35). But since the blood of Christ has been shed, we may draw near to God with full confidence, and as often as we will.

2. Our approach is "by a new and living way" (Hebrews 10:20)

When the Lord was crucified, the veil of the Temple, which had formerly barred the people from the Holiest Place, "the veil of the temple was torn in two from top to bottom" (Matthew 27:51). God was announcing to the world by this miracle that all barriers to his presence were done away by the death of his Son as our Substitute. The old way of approach through an earthly priesthood and animal sacrifice was gone; a new and living way was opened for us.

3. A new welcome is also ours (Hebrews 10:21)

We now have "a high priest over the house of God," the Savior and mediator (1 Timothy 2:5), who is waiting to welcome us to the throne room of the universe when we pray. He has entered within the veil for our sakes, "having become high priest forever" (Hebrews 6:18–20).

In view of this wonderful provision that has been made for us, we are encouraged to draw near to God (v. 22). We are his children. He is delighted to hear our requests and our expressions of gratitude. Not once a year, but "without ceasing" we are to come before him (1 Thessalonians 5:17). With all the riches of divine grace at our disposal; with higher privileges than the Old Testament saints enjoyed under the law; with "exceedingly great and precious promises" freely given (2 Peter 1:4), it is amazing that we take so little advantage of the fact that heaven is always open to the prayer of the Christian.

4. How are we to go into God's presence? (Hebrews 10:22)

a. *"With a true heart"* (v. 22). Hypocrisy, or any sort of religious pretense, marks a prayer as insincere in the sight of God, even though we may fool other people. Christ gave an illustration of this as recorded in Luke 18:10–14. He revealed that the kind of public prayer that comes from a desire to impress others brings no other reward than the dubious one of having the audience admire the language or piety of the speaker (Matthew 6:5).

Several Old Testament rules for acceptable prayer ought to be remembered.

(1) If I regard iniquity in my heart, the Lord will not hear me (Psalm 66:18 NKJV).

To "regard iniquity" is to cherish it, and love it, and be unwilling to give it up for the Lord's sake. As long as anyone persists in some cherished sin, his prayer is unheard.

(2) One who turns away his ear from hearing the law,
Even his prayer is an abomination (Proverbs 28:9
NKJV).

Prayer becomes sin if we refuse to listen to what God's Word has to say to us. This is plain language and may seem unjust to the enemies of the Bible; but we must realize that God is dealing with the root of all the misery and sin in the world today. That sin is unbelief, shown in disobedience of God's Word.

(3) Whoever shuts his ears to the cry of the poor
Will also cry himself and not be heard (Proverbs 21:13
NKJV).

Love is the fulfilling of the law; love is greater than faith and hope (1 Corinthians 13:13).

b. *"In full assurance of faith"* (Hebrews 10:22). Everything has been done to make this possible. God promises to give us our hearts' desires if we delight ourselves in him (Psalm 37:4); "the prayer of the upright is His delight" (Proverbs 15:8). Three New Testament passages exemplify the truth that God wants us to have full assurance as we pray.

(1) If you abide in Me, and My words abide in you,
you will ask what you desire, and it shall be done for
you (John 15:7 NKJV).

Abiding in him is obeying him (v. 10). Allowing his words to abide in us is learning and honoring the teachings of Scripture. These conditions are simple enough for anyone to understand, but they require giving Christ the place human nature wants to reserve for self; therefore not all Christians really know the meaning of this promise and the blessing it offers.

> (2) Beloved, if our heart condemn us not, then have we confidence toward God. And whatsoever we ask, we receive of him, because we keep his commandments, and do those things that are pleasing in his sight (1 John 3:21–22).

Unconfessed, unforsaken sin brings self-condemnation. Obedience to the Lord's commandment (v. 23) is necessary to answered prayer.

> (3) Now this is the confidence that we have in Him, that if we ask anything according to His will, He hears us. And if we know that He hears us, whatever we ask, we know that we have the petitions that we have asked of Him (1 John 5:14–15 NKJV).

Men may try to water this down, but countless believers have found it true. God's Word is his will. Prayer based on what the Scriptures teach and what he reveals to us as his holy will is always answered in the affirmative, even though the answer may seem long delayed (Daniel 10:12–13).

c. *"Having our hearts sprinkled from an evil conscience and our bodies washed with pure water"* (Hebrews 10:22). Two symbols appear in these phrases: sprinkling and washing. The first refers to the heart, or the immaterial part of man; the second refers to the body, the material part of man. The two agencies are blood and water. It should be obvious that neither word is intended in a literal sense. When we pray, the physical application of blood and water is not necessary each time, but the spiritual application of both is required.

Sin is under the blood of sprinkling (Hebrews 9:19–22); therefore we must not be troubled with an evil conscience about past sins. No matter how guilty we once were, we have been cleansed by the blood of the Lamb of God (1 Corinthians 6:9–11).

There is, however, another cleansing agency, the Word of God, so described many times in the Bible (Psalm 119:9; John 17:17). The blood and the Word are mentioned together in Ephesians 5:25–27

> Christ loved the church, and gave himself for it [the blood]; that he might sanctify and cleanse it with the washing of water by the word, that be might present it to himself a glorious church.

THE CHRISTIAN LIFE IS A LIFE OF PUBLIC TESTIMONY

> Let us hold fast the confession of our hope without wavering, for he who promised is faithful (Hebrews 10:23 NASB).

This is equivalent to the phrase in the apostles' creed of Titus 2:13, "looking for the blessed hope." More verses are devoted to the subject of the Lord's return than to any other theme in the New Testament.

"Therefore you also be ready, for the Son of Man is coming at an hour you do not expect," the Lord Jesus said (Matthew 24:44 NKJV). In the parable of the virgins, the oil of the indwelling Holy Spirit, who makes it possible for believers to "shine as lights in the world" (Philippians 2:15; Matthew 5:16), is given great prominence. That parable ends with a warning about the believer's attitude in view of the Lord's return (Matthew 25:1–13).

In Mark 13:34–37 the Lord reiterated the same warning. He gave to every man his *work* (v. 34), commanded all to *watch* (v. 37), and said further that we must wait in expectancy:

> Let your waist be girded and your lamps burning; and you yourselves be like men who wait for their master, when he will return from the wedding, that when he comes and knocks they may open to him immediately. Blessed are those servants whom the master, when he comes, will find watching (Luke 12:35–37 NKJV).

The epistles contain frequent references to our confession of that blessed hope (Titus 2:13). Peter warned that in the last days scoffers would ask:

> Where is the promise of his coming? (2 Peter 3:4 NKJV).

Then he exhorted believers, saying:

> Be diligent to be found by Him in peace, without spot and blameless (3:14 NKJV).

James wrote:

> You also be patient. Establish your hearts, for the coming of the Lord is at hand (James 5:8 NKJV).

John said:

> Everyone who has this hope in Him purifies himself, just as He is pure (1 John 3:3 NKJV).

The church of the Thessalonians is held before us as having given occasion for thanksgiving, because they "turned to God from idols to serve the living and true God, and to wait for His Son from heaven" (1 Thessalonians

1:9–10 NKJV). They were saved from their sin; they were saved to serve God in this present life; and they were saved to wait for the consummation of their hope in the return of the Lord to take them to glory.

This confession of our hope is inseparable from the outward witness of a pure life in the sight of the world. Such a testimony will not waver. He is faithful that promised:

> For yet a little while,
> And He who is coming will come and will not tarry
> (Hebrews 10:37 NKJV).

THE CHRISTIAN LIFE IS A LIFE OF SERVICE TO CHRIST AND HIS CHURCH

> Let us consider one another to provoke unto love and to good works, not forsaking the assembling of our-selves together (Hebrews 10:24–25).

Just as we are to draw near to God in prayer by faith, to witness a good confession before the world as to our hope, so we are to minister to other Christians in love.

> Now abide faith, hope, love, these three; but the greatest of these is love (1 Corinthians 13:13 NKJV).

Christ revealed how we may let all men know that we are his disciples. It is not by telling others how much we pray or how much we know about the Second Coming. It is not even by becoming outstanding students of the Bible, by separating ourselves from sin and false teaching, by religious zeal, by building a better world, or any other thing, no matter how worthy it may seem to us.

135

> By this all will know that you are My disciples, if you
> have love for one another (John 13:35 NKJV).

The original Greek language of Hebrews 10:24 gives us a
picture of believers' fixing their minds attentively on one
another, to take note of one another's spiritual well-being,
with a view to stimulating love and good works. There is
to be mutual care among the members of the church.

A similar thought appears in Philippians 2:3–4(NKJV):

> Let nothing be done through selfish ambition or
> conceit, but in lowliness of mind let each esteem
> others better than himself. Let each of you look out
> not only for his own interests, but also for the interests
> of others.

There are definite obligations resting on us toward one
another, toward the particular church to which we belong, and toward the church universal scattered over the
whole earth. This part of the book of Hebrews evidently
has the local church in view. We are plainly told not to
forsake the assembly of believers, which is the gathering
together of Christians for worship. Neglect of the church
is a serious thing. Immediately following the exhortation
not to forsake the church is a reference to those who sin
willfully after receiving a knowledge of the truth, suggesting
that unnecessary absence from the services of worship in
our church is related to willful sin.

When one goes to church, he gives his influence and
example to everything the church stands for in the community. When he stays away, he is casting his vote in
favor of closing the church as an institution not worthy
of his support. The absentee on Sunday morning is telling
everyone who observes him that he personally does not

care whether or not the church continues to exist as a force for righteousness, a guardian of public morals, a teacher of God's Word, a winner of lost souls, and a rallying place for the people of God. The one who is present is declaring to all who know him and see him going to and from the services that he counts the church important and deserving of his wholehearted support.

Why is it necessary that we do not forsake the assembling of ourselves together? The following are some of the practical benefits derived from the church. There we find Christian fellowship with other believers. There we hear a man of God obeying the injunction, "Preach the Word!" And we find stores of spiritual strength as the pastor unfolds to us the riches of truth in Christ Jesus. We receive teaching on how best to conduct ourselves to achieve the greatest success in life (Joshua 1:8).

Our children there hear of God's love and God's law. We meet older believers who, out of their ripe experience as servants of God, are willing to counsel us. In time of sorrow, there is comfort to be had in the church from Christians who love us and who speak out of a long experience of God's great faithfulness.

In the church we find opportunities to engage in practical Christian service, to engage in a world-wide missionary enterprise, to carry on social work of every sort, to enjoy Christian companionship to the fullest. Ordinarily it is only in the organized body of believers, who carry on the customs of the apostles in obedience to Christ, that we are able to partake of the sacraments of baptism and the Lord's Supper.

There are times when we especially need the church, and there are times when the church especially needs us. The history of organized Christianity shows that spiritual darkness has often descended upon God's people. God's Word was no longer preached from the pulpit or honored in the lives of those who sat in the pew. To those who lived in such a time, when the church had a name that she lived while death really prevailed (Revelation 3:1), the message was given:

> Be watchful, and strengthen the things which remain, that are ready to die (3:2).

SUMMARY

The Christian has recourse to prayer; he must contend earnestly for the faith (Jude 3); he is to carry on a personal soul-winning ministry in tender compassion for those in darkness (Jude 20–23).

As we obey Hebrews 10:25, "not forsaking the assembling of ourselves together, as is the manner of some," we ought to go to church prayerfully, asking God to bless his Word through his minister. If possible we ought to take our friends with us, especially those whom we are seeking to win to Christ. We ought to go bearing the proper share of our tithes and offerings. If we do these things, we shall find the church a source of spiritual refreshment sufficient to brighten and bless our whole week afterward.

12

New Power for the New Life

Faced with the wonderful promises of the Bible and the glorious prospect of living a God-planned life, some Christians wonder whether they can actually stand up against the world, the flesh, and the devil, and emerge victorious. Is there a secret which, if discovered, will enable them not only to overcome temptation, but to please God in everything?

THE POWER FOR VICTORIOUS LIVING

The answer found in the Word of God is astonishing. It thrills the soul of the believer who means business about serving the Lord in the place of his choosing. God has given to his people a supernatural power far greater than the power of their enemies—"the power of the Holy Spirit" (Romans 15:13). It is unlimited, freely available, suited to every situation. The Bible clearly reveals the laws governing the use of this power.

As believers, we are children of God the Father and followers of God the Son. But we are also indwelt by God the Holy Spirit. Christ promised:

> I will pray the Father, and he shall give you another Comforter, that he may abide with you forever; even the Spirit of truth; whom the world cannot receive (John 14:16–17 NKJV).

There is a rich body of Scripture teaching regarding the Spirit. His coming was prophesied centuries before he came to dwell in believers on the day of Pentecost (Joel 2:28; Acts 2:4, 16). He lives within us (1 Corinthians 3:16; 6:19); teaches us (John 14:26); leads us (Romans 8:14); makes intercession for us (Roman 8:26); enables us to be fruitful (Galatians 5:22); convicts those to whom we bear witness (John 16:8); and carries on many other ministries on our behalf. Every such work of the Holy Spirit is worthy of careful study,[1] but our present purpose is to develop only the theme of the power for victorious living that he provides for believers.

1. The extent of this power— more than we can ask or think

In Ephesians 3:20, it is written that God "is able to do

---

1 See *The Person and Work of the Holy Spirit* by René Pache for a more extensive study of the Holy Spirit.

exceeding abundantly above all that we ask or think, according to the power that [works] in us."

We think and pray about many things concerning the promises of God. Yet no matter how daring our thoughts about what we want to accomplish for the Lord; no matter how seemingly impossible the great and mighty things for which we pray (Jeremiah 33:3), he is able to do more than we ask or think. And lest we be inclined to pass this by with the inattention that so often makes ineffective some statement in the Word, our minds are arrested and our spirits are challenged by the revelation that he is able not only to do more than we ask or think, but exceeding abundantly above!

2. The place where this power is exercised—in us

If this were simply a statement about the omnipotence of God, we would hardly consider it in a study of practical truth for life on earth today, but it includes a phrase that brings it right down to where we live, in home or school or the workplace. The ability of God is limited only by "the power that works in us." Here is a phrase with a practical purpose. We are encouraged to count on God's ability to exceed our fondest hopes and expectations. He wants us to succeed in doing his will. He expects us to think more about his ability than our inability.

3. The greatness of this power

Since God is able to do so much according to the power that works in us, it is of surpassing importance that we know what this is. The word translated power in the original is *dunamis*, of which the nearest English equivalent is *dynamic*. It is used many times in the New Testament. Probably the most striking occurrence is in Ephesians 1:19, part of a prayer uttered by the apostle Paul for the Christians in the city of Ephesus, where he had been pastor for three years (Acts 20:31). Even though they had sat under his teaching for so long, there were certain truths he longed to see them know in larger measure. He prayed that their understanding might be enlightened so that they might know three things (Ephesians 1:18), one of which was this:

> what is the exceeding greatness of His power toward us who believe, according to the working of His mighty power (v. 19 NKJV).

Seven expressive words. In this verse there is a piling up of superlatives dealing with the power of God. If this seems strange in our English version, it is even more remarkable in the original language, because there are seven Greek words or roots in the verse, all of which have been brought over into our tongue to express power, quantity, or strength. Even though we may not know a word of Greek, it is instructive to know what these seven words are.

(1) The first of them, in importance, is our word from Ephesians 3:20, *dunamis*, from which come *dynamite* and *dynamo*. One of these is an explosive; the other is a machine for transforming visible mechanical energy into invisible electrical energy. (2) The Greek *energeian* is found in our language in such forms as energy and energetic. (3) The prefix *hyper*, meaning an excess of something, forms the first part of words like *hypertension*. (4) *Kratous* turns up in the last syllable of *autocrat*, a powerful dictator. (5) The strongest bone in the human body is the *ischium*, which sounds like *ischuos*. (6) When radio technicians speak of a *megohm*, they mean a million ohms of resis-

tance, and they draw the word for million from *mega,* found in the verse before us. (7) *Ballo,* to throw forth, is familiar to us in the form of the science of projectiles, called *ballistics.*

It is resurrection power. Any one of these seven words in Ephesians 1:19 would be important by itself; but when all of them are crowded into one verse, it becomes evident that God is seeking to impress us with something tremendous.

While it is true that he is speaking of the power that brought Christ from the dead, he is applying this truth to believers as the power available to Christians today and every day. The part of Ephesians 1:19 that is developed in the following verses is the statement that God's power is to those who believe.

To demonstrate how remarkably true this is, read a few verses of Ephesians in a special way. Omit for a moment the end of chapter one, which speaks of Christ's present exaltation, and the words in italics in 2:1 in the King James Version because they are not found in the original. They were introduced from 2:5 because the translators noticed that there was no verb in verse 1. We therefore read 1:19, the first half of 1:20, and 2:1. In doing so, we are able to see something that otherwise might escape us in the inspired text.

The apostle Paul is praying that believers may know "the working of his mighty power, which he wrought in Christ, when he raised him from the dead" (Ephesians 1:19–20). The same divine power that brought Christ forth from the tomb also brought us forth from our death in sin when we were given everlasting life upon believing in Christ! (2:1).

This is, of course, not the only place where we read that

our salvation is far more than some have supposed it to be, some who think of it only as a form of religion, or a commendable manifestation of brotherhood. In Romans 1:16 the apostle said:

> I am not ashamed of the gospel of Christ, for it is the power of God to salvation for everyone who believes (NASB).

This, again, is our word *dunamis*, which also appears in 1 Corinthians 1:18, "The preaching of the cross is to them that perish foolishness; but unto us which are saved it is the power of God."

It is creation power. Here is a truth that helps us to understand why Ephesians 2:10 refers to Christians as "his workmanship, created in Christ Jesus unto good works"; and why 2 Corinthians 5:17 (NKJV) declares:

> If anyone is in Christ, he is a new creation: old things have passed away; behold, all things have become new.

If we have a weak concept of what is involved in salvation, we cannot understand the greatness of the power of God, which, according to his purpose, must be working in us to enable us to accomplish his will.

When God saves a soul, there is a manifestation of creative power. It is not too much to say that it is a greater demonstration of his power than was seen in the creation of the world. Psalm 8:3 speaks of the heavens as the work of his fingers; but Isaiah 52:10 (NKJV) declares:

> The Lord has made bare His holy arm In the eyes of all the nations;

144

And all the ends of the earth shall see
The salvation of our God.

This is a most amazing contrast. Salvation requires that God make bare the arm of his creative power. "The arm of the LORD" is revealed to those who believe the report contained in his Word (Isaiah 53:1). Comparatively few verses speak of his creating the heavens and the earth, while many books of the Bible are devoted to the salvation of the perishing human race, which required the death of God's Son on the cross.

THE BIBLE—
PROOF OF THE POWER OF THE HOLY SPIRIT

For further light upon "the power that works in us," we should examine the promise of Christ and the prayers and the preaching of the apostles.

1. Promised by the risen Lord

As the time drew near for the fulfillment of Old Testament prophecies regarding the coming of the Holy Spirit, the crucified and risen Son of God confirmed these prophecies with his own promise:

Behold, I send the Promise of My Father upon you; but tarry in the city of Jerusalem until you are endued with power from on high" (Luke 24:49 NKJV).

These are the last words of Christ before his ascension to heaven to be recorded in the gospel of Luke. A similar promise is found in Acts 1:8 (NKJV):

You shall receive power when the Holy Spirit has come upon you; and you shall be witnesses to Me.

2. Bestowed at Pentecost

The second chapter of Acts bears abundant testimony to the transformation that took place in the disciples after the promised power came upon them at Pentecost. Peter, the timid fisherman who had feared the words of a maid (Luke 22:54–57), now fearlessly declared the message of God. Three thousand people believed and were baptized. This power promised by Christ is the power that works in us today. It has been manifesting itself through the church ever since Pentecost. It has never been diminished or withdrawn, even though unbelief or ignorance may often have prevented its manifestation.

There is an interesting progress of thought here. In Psalm 62:11 it is written, "Power belongs to God." As we turn the pages of the Bible, we read in Matthew 28:18 that the risen Lord said, "All power is given unto me in heaven and in earth." Then in Acts 1:8 his further promise is given, "You shall receive power." And Ephesians 3:20 speaks of the "power that works in us." That which belonged to God was given to Christ. He transmitted it to us, and it is his purpose that it shall enable us to do exploits for God.

3. Recognized in the apostles' prayers

God's power is mentioned in the promise of Christ; it is found also in the prayers of the apostles. We have already noticed the prayer of Paul in Ephesians 1. Lest we misunderstand what it is and assume that each of us is to become a flaming evangelist or a great Bible teacher or missionary, we should read carefully Colossians 1:11. This verse contains a prayer that we be "strengthened with all might, according to his glorious power, unto all patience

146

and longsuffering with joyfulness." The power of God is just as much in evidence when a humble Christian manifests patience or longsuffering or joy, as when a highly gifted believer moves a large congregation by his preaching. The promise of Christ is fulfilled in us, and the prayers of the apostles are answered when the power of God works in us.

4. Experienced by the apostles

One more series of passages should be mentioned, those passages which speak of the practice and the preaching of the apostles. Paul said in Colossians 1:29 (NKJV):

> I also labor, striving according to His working which works in me mightily.

That is, in his own service he was conscious of the practical experience of Ephesians 3:20. God was working in him "both to will and to do for his good pleasure" (Philippians 2:13). This should be our normal experience.

In their preaching and testifying, "with great power gave the apostles witness of the resurrection of the Lord Jesus" (Acts 4:33). With perfect naturalness, Paul was able to say to one of the churches where he had been:

> Our gospel came not unto you in word only, but also in power, and in the Holy [Spirit] (1 Thessalonians 1:5).

If our witness today is less powerful, it is only because we have departed from the apostolic pattern; for God is still able to do far more than we ask or think, if we let his power work in us.

How the Power of the Holy Spirit Works Through Us

How, then, do we utilize this power? What is the secret that can transform an ordinary mortal into an instrument of God, the channel through which supernatural power can flow for the blessing of the world?

1. We must die

In the physical world, we must obey natural laws if we want the forces of nature to work for us. For example, a tremendous advance in civilization followed the discovery of the laws governing the use of steam. Throughout the centuries electrical power was waiting to be used, but men were unable to take advantage of it until the laws of electrical energy were studied and obeyed. The use of atomic power had to await the discovery of laws controlling the atom.

In the spiritual world also there are definite laws governing "the power that works in us." One passage in particular demands our attention, a statement by the apostle Paul expressing his longing to know God's power in a richer, deeper, fuller way. His prayer was

> that I may know him, and the power of his resurrection, and the fellowship of his sufferings, being made conformable unto his death (Philippians 3:10).

This was written nearly thirty years after Paul's experience on the Damascus Road. He had served God faithfully, had wrought great things for God, had demonstrated what could be accomplished through a man who wholly followed his Lord, even though he was in "bodily presence . . . weak" (2 Corinthians 10:10).

Even after such a life, what did the apostle want most? To know Christ and the power of his resurrection. Once more we find that he uses the word *dunamis*, to which Ephesians 3:20 introduced us. If Paul felt a continuing need for this power, surely we cannot get along without it!

We have already seen that the power of Christ's resurrection is the power of the Holy Spirit entrusted to believers at Pentecost and working through them ever since. Paul now reminds us that resurrection power is inseparable from crucifixion. What does this mean, to be made conformable unto Christ's death? It means being able to say with Paul:

> I have been crucified with Christ; it is no longer I who live, but Christ lives in me; and the life which I now live in the flesh I live by faith in the Son of God, who loved me and gave Himself for me (Galatians 2:20 NKJV).

A look at the verses preceding Philippians 3:10 makes it clear that this meant, for Paul, far more than a pious platitude. He had known many worldly advantages, but he counted them loss for Christ (v. 7). More than this, he regarded them as refuse, and had actually given them all up for Christ, for whom he had "suffered the loss of all things" (v. 8).

We may not be called upon, as he was, to leave everything we have known of comfort and personal advantage (although many missionaries do so); but we are certainly called upon to die to anything that stands between us and our Lord. What does it mean to die to such things? How do we do this? Surely such an important key to the outflow of the power of the Spirit is not left without clear teaching as to how a Christian may experience this power. Sometimes one meets sincere believers who know that the Bible speaks of their being crucified with Christ and are honestly trying to die to some fleshly habit, yet without success. No matter how hard they try to persuade themselves that they are victorious, they continue to suffer defeat.

2. The threefold secret of victorious living

God never intended that we should try to die to sin. He knows that we would fail if that were the way to victory. Instead, he gave a very simple, threefold truth that frees us from the bondage of sin so that we may enjoy the fullness of the power of the Holy Spirit. This truth takes the entire problem of sin out of the area of self-effort and puts it in the hands of God himself. It is found in Romans 6, and it is so simple that we may not consider it important unless we accept it as truly from God.

Know what God has said. The first part of this threefold secret of a victorious life has to do with *knowledge* of what God has said. Three times we read of *knowing* something on the authority of the Bible. We *know* that we have been united with Christ in such a way that, in the sight of God, we died with the Lord Jesus on the cross. We do not have to understand how this can be; we simply accept it as true because God said it. We also know that our "old man"—all that we were before we were saved—was crucified with him, that "we should not serve sin" (Romans 6:6). Finally,we know that when Christ died, he died unto sin, was raised from the dead, and now lives unto God.

These revealed facts underlie God's plan to provide victory and power for us. They are forever settled. The

Bible says they are true. By faith we accept them, for faith is simply believing God.

Reckon it true. The second part of our threefold secret is found in verse 11:

> Likewise reckon . . . also yourselves to be dead indeed unto sin, but alive unto God through Jesus Christ our Lord.

Here the important word is *reckon* which means to count as true. We start with the belief that we died with Christ; then, when we are tempted to sin, we count upon this as actually true. Instead of *trying* to die to sin (a form of self-effort in which we never could succeed), we rely upon the fact that in Christ we have already died to sin.

The facts are true whether, in our own experience, we reckon them so or not. When faced with the temptation to sin, we remember that we died to sin in Christ; and it therefore has no power over us. We are dead to sin and alive unto God.

Yield to God. The third great word appears in verse 13:

> Yield yourselves unto God, as those that are alive from the dead, and your members as instruments of righteousness unto God.

Reckoning may be said to be an act of the mind; yielding is an act of the will. Yielding to God is necessary if we are to derive practical value from our reckoning that what God says of us is true. We surrender to him and present our bodies to God (Romans 12:1–2).

Thus Romans 6 tells us how the truth that we are crucified with Christ can become an actual daily dying to sin. This conformity to Christ's death is the true secret of knowing "him and the power of his resurrection." God's power, working in us, enables him to do exceeding abundantly above all we ask or think.

3. *Victorious living*

We dare not despise this simple threefold key to the power of the Spirit. Are these three words not also the key to the release of the forces of nature? For example, how was the first electric motor invented, making electrical power available to mankind? First, there had to be *knowledge* of the basic truths governing electrical force, discovered by research. Without knowledge, no other steps could be taken. Second, it was necessary to reckon on the practical usefulness of what was known. It had to be counted as true, depended upon as changeless natural law that would work in a mechanism devised to use it. Third, in his actual design, the inventor had to yield to what was known. He could not introduce his own will, or anything contrary to known natural laws. It became necessary for him to yield, or surrender, to known truth if be was to he successful in getting this natural force to work for him.

It is only as we know what God has revealed, in faith reckon it to be true of us, and *yield* ourselves to God, that we can expect to see the supernatural power of God working through us.

I one day met a great missionary leader and asked him, "What was the greatest spiritual experience of your life?" The missionary replied, "During the early years of my Christian life I lived in defeat. I had no power with God or with men. Knowing that the Bible said I was crucified with Christ, I honestly tried to die to every known sin and weakness, but victory over sin eluded me. Then one day I discovered the wonderful simplicity of the sixth chapter of Romans. I saw that God did not ask me to try to die to sin, or to achieve victory by my own effort. Instead, I was simply to reckon on the truth of what God said: I died with Christ, and therefore I died to sin. When I began to rest in this truth, I entered into such joy and victory and power that it transformed my life. I date my usefulness to God from the wonderful day when I began to believe God's Word, and ceased to try to do something which had already been done for me."

The threefold secret of Romans 6 worked for that missionary, as it has worked for countless others. It will work for us if we will let it.

Devotional Guide

How to Have a Quiet Time

The Word of God. As you read your Bible day by day, remember that it is God's Word and that it should be read thoughtfully and prayerfully. Before beginning your Quiet Time, even as you open your Bible at the day's portion, bow your head in prayer. Why not use the words of the psalmist? "Open my eyes, that I may see wondrous things from Your law" (Psalm 119:18).

Read carefully the Scripture portion, weighing each word. Then read the note for the day, looking up the verses to which special reference is made. Finally, use the following eight-question check. Ask yourself if you can find . . .

1. An example to follow
2. A command to obey
3. A promise to rely on
4. A warning to take note of
5. A prayer to use as your own
6. The main lesson
7. The best verse
8. Something new about the Christian life

Out of each day's reading, choose a verse or a few words to think about during the day; and learn at least one verse a week by heart. Keep a notebook or diary and record something about which God has spoken to you each day. Every true impression should be capable of expression.

The Word with God. Take the message God has given you in your Quiet Time and turn it into a prayer. Ask the Lord to conform your will to his. Then, perhaps using a prayer list, begin to pray for others, asking that God will make real in their experience the truths he has revealed to you. Share your burdens and problems, your hopes and ambitions, with your heavenly Father. Ask him to show you his "good, and acceptable, and perfect will" (Romans 12:2) in relation to all these circumstances. Seek his blessing on the day and his strength to live according to his will.

The Word for God. Share the blessing of your Quiet Time with someone else during the day. As the Lord Jesus opens doors for you, tell others what he means to you. Translate into obedience whatever he has commanded you through your reading of his Word.

FIRST WEEK
Studies in the Life of Abraham

Sunday: Genesis 12:1–9

Abraham's first big step. God revealed the first step in his plan for Abraham. For Abraham, following God meant a complete break from the comfortable, secure life of Ur or Haran. It meant trusting himself absolutely to the invisible security of God's guidance and provision. "He went out, not knowing where he was going" (Hebrews 11:8).

This was for Abraham the beginning of a life of faith. Have you taken your first step yet? Only when Abraham obeyed did he begin to realize what great plans God had for his life (see v. 7).

Monday: Genesis 13: 1–11

Through testing times. Verse 2 does not look like a very big test for Abraham! Yet it speaks of something which has ruined many people's walk of faith. Your testing may come in some quite different way. But let Abraham's answer be your answer too (v. 4). Constant fellowship with the Lord will keep you true. Never fail to call upon him daily. Notice how Abraham's character shows the result of this fellowship with God in a very practical way. His generous self-denial averts a serious quarrel (vv. 8–9).

Tuesday: Genesis 13:12–18

Spiritual riches are best. To be cut off from the rich land of the plains and confined to the hill country was a serious blow, materially, for Abraham. But God had some better promise to give him (vv. 14–16). You see, Abraham was still right in the center of God's plan for him; therefore he was "rich toward God" (Luke 12:21). Lot's life, on the other hand, proved to be useless and disastrous after his prayerless choice of the plain of Jordan. Twice he had to be rescued from captivity or destruction, and his life achieved nothing for God.

Wednesday: Genesis 17:1–8

Waiting! God had promised Abraham that his descendants would inherit the land and that all nations of the earth would be blessed through him. But at ninety-nine years of age, Abraham still had no son and heir! How long had he now been waiting? (compare 12:4). Therefore, to encourage him, God repeats his promise, calling it a covenant (a solemn agreement). What a large part waiting seems to play in God's plan for us! What must we do while we are waiting for the next step? (see v. 1).

Thursday: Genesis 21:1–8

The reward of faith. "The Lord did . . . as He had spoken" (v. 1). When lives are in his hands without reserve God can and will fulfill his cherished purposes. "At the set time . . ." (v. 2). God's timing is always perfect, however slow his ways may seem to us in our impatience. "God has made me laugh" (v. 6)—the laugh of amazement and joy at what God can do with human weakness. "Who would have said. . . ?" (v. 7). Who could guess even now what God will do through your life if you will give him the chance?

Friday: Genesis 22:1–10

"God will provide" (v. 8). What! Is there to be still more testing? Yes, the greatest honor God pays to any man is to test him through suffering (Hebrews 12:6). The faith of a true servant of God is tested to the very end of his life. Here God seems to be asking Abraham to renounce the aim and purpose of his whole life—his son Isaac, the child of promise. Abraham's faith is well summed up in three words: "My son, God. . . ." Let the will and glory of God be your one desire, and offer up all your other aims to him.

Saturday: Genesis 22:11–19

"You . . . have not withheld" (v. 16). This is God's commendation of his servant Abraham—nothing withheld!

God's plan never led Abraham to a more terrible place than Mount Moriah, where life seemed to crumble about him. Yet he followed faithfully; perplexed, troubled, but still trusting and still following. And from the darkest depths God brought the fullest blessing. We too must be willing to sacrifice our greatest treasures. But what less could we give to him who "did not spare his own Son, but delivered Him up for us all" (Romans 8:32)?

Second Week
Key Teachings from the Sermon on the Mount

Sunday: Matthew 5:1–16

Character first! Our preoccupation is often with the questions: "What does God want me to do?" "Where does God want me to go?" However, God's first interest is in what our *character* is like. Thus, before we can act as salt in the world, we must have a true savor ourselves (v. 13); before the city is seen, it must be built; before the candle can shine, it must be lit; and before men will glorify our Father, they must see our good works (vv. 14–16). Test yourself honestly by Christ's standard (vv. 3–10). Turn each verse into prayer.

Monday: Matthew 5:38–48

"You have heard . . . but I tell you. . . . " Christian living is to be on a far higher moral level than anyone else has either said (vv. 38, 43) or done (vv. 46–47). In verses 38–42 the emphasis is on the fact that there must be no limit to the self-sacrifice we will endure for others' sake; then in verses 43–47 Christ teaches that this love must be shown to

all, whatever their attitude to us may have been. Verse 48 is the final challenge. Will you begin living this life now?

Tuesday: Matthew 6:1–15

Whose approval do you want? God's or men's? You can rarely have both, you know. To seek the one is to lose the other (vv. 1, 6), and deeds done for men's eyes earn no divine approval (vv. 2, 5). Notice the prayer that pleases God. It is *secret* (v. 6), a private interview with the heavenly Father. It is *sincere* (v. 7) springing from the heart, not just the lips. It is *simple* (vv. 9–13), bringing praises and prayers one by one before God. Give your own prayer life this threefold test.

Wednesday: Matthew 6:16–24

Where is your treasure? If we are to know God's will for our lives, there is another snare to be avoided. Verses 19–21 describe the snare and the reason it is dangerous. One can profess to seek the Lord's will while his heart is elsewhere. He must have a "single eye" to the heavenly treasure of our Lord's "Well done!" (v. 22). A Christian who has not renounced all ambition for material things is like a man vainly trying to please two masters (v. 24). Let all your treasure be above (v. 20).

Thursday: Matthew 6:25–34

"Your heavenly Father knows . . ." (v. 32). Verses 19–24 warned us against ambition for material things. Today's portion speaks of anxiety for them. Not only must we not *seek* for riches, but also we must not worry about whether we shall have enough to meet our needs. Verse 33 tells us what we should be concerned about, and then gives us a promise to claim at all times. To step out thus in obedience

to God demands faith. "Little faith" (v. 30) will fail to prove God's provision.

Friday: Matthew 7:1–12

Two more essentials. Here are two more things we must learn if we are to be effective for God: (a) We must learn *not to judge.* Harsh criticism is constantly used by Satan to break up Christian unity and fellowship. We must be humble, holy, and helpful (vv. 1–5). (b) We must learn *to intercede.* The Christian worker who does not live by intercession will have a fruitless life. Only those who are constantly asking will constantly receive (vv. 7–11). Do not be afraid to persevere in prayer!

Saturday: Matthew 7:13–29

Make sure he knows you! Yes, make sure Christ knows you as one of his own. Many people who call him "Lord," who have done much so-called Christian work, and who have even preached in his name, will be turned away as being counterfeit Christians (vv. 21–23). We must make sure now that we have entered in at the narrow gate (vv. 13 and 14), that we are good trees (vv. 17–20), and that we are building on the Rock, Jesus Christ (vv. 24–27). Have you received him as Savior? Are you doing his will? Does he know you? (see verse 23).

THIRD WEEK
"Faithful unto Death"
Two Stories from Daniel

Sunday: Daniel 3:1–7

Worship or die! Nebuchadnezzar's foolish whim presented the three children of God (v. 12) with the greatest possible test of their faith. *It was unforeseeable!* A dedication ceremony (v. 2) was suddenly changed into a scene of heathen worship (vv. 4–6). The test came when the children of God least expected it. *It was unavoidable!* "At that time" the band began to play (v. 7). They had no time to plan what they would do, or even to consult together. It is at such times that our faith is really seen for what it is.

Monday: Daniel 3:8–15

The demand to conform. Worldly society hates those who will not conform to its ways. The Christian who is "different" will always be the subject of gossip and criticism (compare v. 8). Pressure will be put upon him to do as everyone else does (v. 15). What must his answer be? (See Romans 12:2.) If he is to win others for Christ, it will not be through imitating their ways but by a triumph of pure Christian character. He may, as the three Jews were, be called upon to go through fiery trials, but he must not flinch.

Tuesday: Daniel 3:16–23

"But if not . . ." (v. 18). The three friends had made up their minds that it was better to die than to sin. Have you? (Compare Hebrews 12:4.) They knew that their God was able to deliver them (v. 17). But would he? They felt sure he would (v. 17). But even if not, even if God did not set free their physical bodies, they were determined not to deny him (v. 18). (See Job 13:15.) God does not always set us free from our troubles, but he always gives us all the strength needed to triumph over them. What did Paul discover in 2 Corinthians 12:7–9?

162

Wednesday: Daniel 3:24–30

The fourth Man. It was in the very flames of testing that the Son of God came close to the three servants, and they came to know him as never before. He was "walking" with them "in the midst of the fire," and "they are not hurt" (v. 25). (a) *The Savior revealed.* Expect suffering to bring you a closer walk with Christ. (b) *The Savior honored.* Through their faithfulness and fortitude others acknowledged God's supremacy: "There is no other God that can deliver like this" (vv. 28–29). Is he honored through you?

Thursday: Daniel 6:1–10

"No charage or fault" (v. 4). What an example to us is this man Daniel (a) *His great holiness.* Even before his enemies his life was faultless and faithful (v. 4). What a testimony was wrung from the lips of these enemies (v. 5)! Would your enemies say this of you? The secret is in verse 3. What is the "excellent spirit"? (See Ezekiel 36:27.) (b) *His good habit.* "He knelt down on his knees three times that day . . . as was his custom" (v. 10). This was not just mechanical! Make for yourself a good spiritual routine for each day and do not break it.

Friday: Daniel 6:11–18

The triumph of evil. Daniel is accused, tried, convicted, sentenced to death, and cast to the lions. Every attempt to frustrate the wicked designs fails (vv. 14–15). The great stone on the mouth of the den apparently buries all hope for Daniel (v. 17). But even when things are at their worst, God has his plans. Do you remember another great stone, one that was supposed to seal Satan's greatest victory? (See Matthew 27:66.) What did God do about it? (See Matthew

28:2.) *As long as we are true to him,* his purposes cannot fail.

Saturday: Daniel 6:19–28

The triumph of God. "Daniel," cried the king, "has your God been . . . able to deliver you?" Daniel replied, "My God sent his angel and shut the lions' mouths" (vv. 20–22). Two qualities in Daniel made this possible: (a) *Innocency* (v. 22). God cannot vindicate his people's sins! This would bring him no glory. (b) *Faith* (v. 23b). The child of God must claim the power God offers, as Daniel did. The result was that Darius saw that God was "the living God" (v. 26) who "works" (v. 27).

FOURTH WEEK
Personal Encounters with Jesus

Sunday: Luke 7:1–10

Come in humility! "Lord . . . I am not worthy" (v. 6). The testimony of others was that he was worthy (v. 4)! How can this be explained? Quite simply: a sense of personal unworthiness is the only thing that makes one "worthy" to come to Christ. Note that this must be a genuine humility, not just a matter of words. The centurion did not even dare to show himself publicly. Loud professions of one's own humility can sometimes be an expression of pride! Compare Luke 18:13 and test yourself.

Monday: Luke 7:11–17

Come in helplessness! Nothing could be more helpless or hopeless than a dead man (v. 12). He could not hear; he could not repent; he could not exercise faith. He could do nothing. Yet his very helplessness pleaded silently for him, and the Lord took action (v. 14). What a change! The man "who was dead sat up and began to speak" (v. 15). Now turn to Ephesians 2:1. We are spiritually dead before we come to Jesus! Let us come to him as we are, that we may be made alive.

Tuesday: Luke 7:18–28

Come in sincerity! Do not act a part, or pretend to be something you are not. If you have problems, confess them frankly, so that Christ may show you the answer. John did the right thing with his doubts (v. 19). He did not brood over them and let them make his heart bitter. He sent them to Jesus for treatment. Spiritual problems are nothing to be ashamed of; they came to John, of whom the Lord said, "There is not a greater prophet" (v. 28). You will find that the answer to all questions is basically the same: the greatness and goodness of our Savior (v. 22).

Wednesday: Luke 7:36–50

Come in penitence! "She is a sinner," said the Pharisee. And he was right, for she was (vv. 37, 39). But then, so was he (see Romans 3:23). Yet there was a difference: (a) *She was a penitent sinner* (v. 38). She had seen her sins for what they were and had turned from them. Simon neither saw his sin nor repented of it. (b) *She was a forgiven sinner* (v. 47). She came to Jesus and heard his gracious word of pardon (v. 48). The Pharisee, for all his fine religion, was yet in his sins.

Thursday: Luke 8:19–25

Come in desperation! Jesus' mother and brothers came

formally, on a family visit (vv. 19–21). Apparently Jesus refused to see them; his time was fully taken up with those in real need. The disciples, on the other hand, came to him with a matter of life and death (vv. 22–25). He immediately answered their request and rebuked the storm. His words, "Where is your faith?" do not criticize their coming to him; they criticize their faithless statement, "We are perishing" (v. 4). Let your every need drive you to Jesus.

Friday: Luke 8:41–48

Come in faith! What! Is this fearful, trembling woman to be taken as an example of faith? What did Jesus say in verse 48? Here is encouragement for us. Saving faith does not need to be spectacular faith. This woman's faith was expressed in three simple ways: (a) *She saw her need* (v. 43). She had proved that there was no human answer to it. (b) *She believed in Jesus* (v. 44). She believed that he was able to heal her. (c) *She came to him* (vv. 44, 47). She put out her hand and made contact. The steps to salvation are just the same.

Saturday: Luke 8:49–56

Come in extremity! The ruler's material prosperity and social position faded into insignificance beside the crushing blow that had fallen on him in the death of his little daughter. Throwing prestige to the winds, he prostrated himself at Jesus' feet before the whole crowd (v. 41) and besought him to come quickly. Nothing mattered at that moment but that he should find Jesus and bring him to his need. He did not plead in vain (v. 50). His prayer was granted (vv. 54–55). Let nothing you have, are, or hope to be keep you from Christ.

FIFTH WEEK
Readings from the Proverbs of Solomon

Sunday: Proverbs 1:1–19

How to be wise. The Book of Proverbs is full of good, sound advice on how to be a wise and instructed child of God. Notice three truths: (a) *The importance of right aims* (vv. 1–6). Some Christians seem almost proud of their ignorance ("I'm just a simple believer). But every Christian should be an instructed Christian. (b) *The importance of right beginnings* (vv. 7–9). A holy fear of the mighty God is the starting point. Wisdom that disregards him is but foolishness. (c) *The importance of right company* (vv. 10–19). Wisdom is God's way, not man's (16:25).

Monday: Proverbs 2:1–9

Seeking and finding. The way to become a wise Christian includes desire (v. 1), *study* (v. 2), *prayer* (v. 3), and *persistence* (v. 4). But even all these would be useless unless the Lord did *his* part. He must reveal truth to you (v. 6), store it in your mind (v. 7), and show you its application in your life (v. 8). You have your part to play, and God has his. Remember also that this "wisdom" is not a dry accumulation of ancient facts, but a growing and vital knowledge of the living Christ (Colossians 2:3, 2 Peter 3:18).

Tuesday: Proverbs 3:1–18

What is a wise man like? We can gather much from these verses about the nature of true, God-given wisdom. It is *pure* (vv. 1–4), forming beautiful character where it abides. It is *purposeful* (vv. 5–8), for it springs from a desire that God's will shall be pre-eminent. It is *practical* (vv. 9–10),

167

leading to right handling of the material aspects of life. It is *patient* (vv. 11–12), for it sees the hand of God behind all circumstances. It is *precious* (vv. 13–18), for it gives joy, peace, and life. (Compare James 3:13–18.)

Wednesday: Proverbs 6:6–19

Watch these weaknesses! "Wisdom" warns us against faults of character. Slothfulness is the subject of verses 6–11. The busy ant should teach a lesson to those with a tendency to laziness (v. 6)! She is active, but it is always activity with a careful purpose (v. 8). In verses 12–15 we are warned against being smart. God does not admire this kind of person, however clever he may appear to others. Finally, look at verses 16–19, a list of weaknesses. Which of these "abominations" do you find within yourself?

Thursday: Proverbs 10:11–22

Let's examine your tongue! The "wise man" is often revealed by his use of his tongue, and the fool also shows himself for what he is. The foolish person's speech is crude and vulgar (v. 11); it provokes argument (v. 12); it is not helpful (v. 13); it leads others away from God (v. 14); it contains lies and harmful remarks about others (v. 18). The fool is always making himself heard (v. 19), but there is little thought behind what he says (vv. 20–21). Now seek out for yourself what is said about the wise man's speech. What makes it rich (v. 22)?

Friday: Proverbs 14:12–27

"A fountain of life" (v. 27). "Wisdom" and "foolishness" in the Book of Proverbs do not refer to the amount of education (even Christian education) one has. They are concerned with progress in holiness and knowledge of the

Lord. By this wisdom, the wise man is able to make a spiritual success of each day. For example, he will walk in the right way (v. 12) and have inner satisfaction (v. 14); he will live prudently (v. 15) and righteously (v. 16). The Lord is a constant refuge for him and his family (v. 26). The wise man has an abundant life (John 10:10).

Saturday: Proverbs 15:1–17

Living thoughtfully. The wise man does not live thoughtlessly; he knows that even the little details of life are important in God's sight. So he takes care that every answer he gives is helpful (v. 1), for example, and that he pays attention to reproof (v. 5), whether it comes from God or man. He cultivates reality, for God sees the heart (vv. 3, 11). His prayer is genuine (v. 8), and his joy is deep—so different from the superficial joviality of the fool (v. 13; 14:13). Are you like this, or do you feed "on foolishness" (v. 14)?

SIXTH WEEK
The Passion of Jesus Christ

Sunday: Mark 8:27–38

The way of the cross. (a) The Savior must be confessed. His death would mean nothing if he were not the Christ. John the Baptist's death could not atone for sin! (v. 28) (b) *The Savior must be crucified.* Only the death and resurrection of Christ could save (v. 31). The way of the cross was God's way; all others were Satan's (v. 33). (c) *The Savior must be crowned.* His Lordship and leadership must be accepted. We must be prepared to follow the example of his death

(vv. 34–38). The life that puts self-preservation first will perish fruitlessly (v. 35).

Monday: Mark 10:32–45

Servant of all. The two disciples wanted to share the "glory" of the Son of God in his kingdom (v. 37). What they did not realize was that his glory would be won only through suffering and death, followed by resurrection (v. 34). Jesus tried to explain it to them (v. 38), but neither they nor the other ten really understood what he was saying (v. 41). We must be sure that we understand it. It is only through death to self that we can be of any true service to others or to our Lord (vv. 44–45).

Tuesday: Mark 11:1–11

A King on a colt! Have you ever considered what a picture this was? (a) *The King.* The people cried, "Blessed is the King who comes in the name of the Lord" (Luke 19:38); and they spread garments and palm branches in the way. It was a scene of regal splendor. (b) *The colt.* The Lord of glory deliberately chose this humble way to present himself as King. Why? Because for our sakes he took the form of a servant. (Compare Matthew 21:5 with Philippians 2:7.)

Wednesday: Mark 14:32–46

No other way. There is a sense in which the battle of Calvary was won in the Garden of Gethsemane. Here Christ discovered that there was no other "possible" way (v. 35) for men to be redeemed. Here he reached his final decision that his Father's will should be done (v. 36). Christ had won the victory in his own soul. Now he could say, "Rise, let us be going" (v. 42). If you are to make progress with the Lord, you will have to fight many battles within your own heart. Get alone, and get on your knees!

Thursday: Mark 14:55–65

"A time to keep silence . . ." (Ecclesiastes 3:7). Christ was not interested in defending his reputation. He "answered nothing" (v. 61). So with the Christian who would follow in his steps. He must lay aside all desire for the approval of men at the sacrifice of God's approval. *"And a time to speak!"* Christ kept silence when false accusations were being hurled against him—but not when his testimony to the truth was concerned, even though to speak then meant certain death! (v. 62). Notice the difference carefully. Keep quiet about yourself; but speak about him.

Friday: Mark 15:1–20

"Crucify him!" All of mankind is rejecting God in the flesh. The Jews cried for Jesus to be crucified (vv. 13–14). Pilate "delivered Jesus . . . to be crucified" (v. 15). The soldiers "led Him out to crucify Him" (v. 20). Rich and poor, Jew and Gentile, East and West, ruler and subject, religionist and pagan, man and woman—all agreed on one thing: "Let him be crucified" (Matthew 27:22). You and I were represented there; we too are guilty (Romans 3:19). Let us humbly repent.

Saturday: Mark 15:21–39

The darkest hour. The darkness began to gather at the sixth hour. By the ninth hour the horror became unbearable, and the cry of verse 34 was wrung from our Lord's lips. It was the agony of separation from the Father, which he had never for a moment experienced before. It was in that terrible ninth hour that he was "stricken, smitten by

God, and afflicted" (Isaiah 53:4). This, not the nails through hands and feet, was the deepest suffering of the crucifixion. This was the "taste" of death spoken of in Hebrews 2:9.

SEVENTH WEEK
From the Life of Paul, Part 1

Sunday: Acts 9:1–9

Begin at the beginning! The only place any Christian biography can begin is with a true conversion. (a)*The Lord was seen.* Paul's first question was, "Who are You, Lord?" (v. 5). He needed first to "know the Lord" as Redeemer and personal Savior. (b) *The life was surrendered.* His second question? "Lord, what do You want me to do?" (v. 6). It must follow naturally if the Lord has been truly seen. He gave; now we must give (Romans 12:1).

Monday: Acts 9:10–19

"*A chosen vessel of Mine.*" Paul is now converted. Ananias calls him "Brother Saul" (v. 17). But this is not the end! (a) *God has a purpose for him.* "He is a chosen vessel" (v. 15). So it is for everyone he brings to Christ. He has a purpose for you, and he will reveal it: "I will show him . . ." (v. 16). (b) *God has a provision for him.* He can "be filled with the Holy Ghost" (v. 17). Yield your life to him today and claim the provision Paul had. Then let every day be lived "for [his] name's sake" (v. 16).

Tuesday: Acts 9:20–30

The humbling continues. The breaking of his pride began long before, with the pricking of his conscience (v. 5). Then there was the time when his vision of the Savior hurled him on his face to the ground (v. 4). Now we see Paul hounded as a criminal, and let down over the wall of Damascus in a basket (v. 25). He never forgot this humiliating experience. Even years later he referred to it (see 2 Corinthians 11:32–33). Let God humble you and bring you to the point where you too can say: "I havea been crucified with Christ" (Galatians 2:20).

Wednesday: Acts 13:1–5

A lesson in guidance. There are some important lessons in discovering the Lord's will here. (a) *Patience.* Look at God's promise in Acts 9:6. Ten years have passed and only now does God fulfill his Word. God is not in a hurry, so you too must have patience. (b) *Preparation.* There was no idleness during the waiting period. Saul and Barnabas were in Christian fellowship and engaged in Christian work (vv. 1–2). (c) *Prayer.* Since the Holy Ghost calls (v. 2) and sends (v. 4), there is no guidance without prayer (v. 3).

Thursday: Acts 14:1–7

Division! The Lord Jesus is so precious to us that it comes as a shock that anyone should want to reject him or his will. But the one who is walking in God's will soon discovers that there will be opposition and division (vv. 2, 4). Paul's own kinsmen, the Jews, formed part of the opposition (v. 5). You too may find those nearest and dearest to you resenting your service for the Lord. You are only sharing the experience of Christ himself (see John 7:43). The right answer is to be bold (v. 3) and faithful (v. 7).

Friday: Acts 14:8–18

A danger and a denial. The danger here is quite different from that in Iconium (v. 5). There it was physical; here it is spiritual. There the body was attacked; here the soul. But behind each danger is Satan himself. Do not suppose that worship of men belongs only to times of paganism, such as are described in verses 11–13. Hero worship is as common today as ever. If you are successful in Christian service (v. 10) you will meet it. What was Paul's attitude? (See v. 15; Romans 12:3.)

Saturday: Acts 14:19–28

"Work . . . completed" (v. 26). (a) *Suffering had been endured* (v. 19). Paul counted it a privilege when he was called upon to suffer for his Master and Lord (compare 1 Peter 4:12–13). (b) *Souls had been won* (v. 20). "Disciples" were now to be found where but a few days before there had been none! And they were disciples with a care for a fellow servant. (c) *Saints had been strengthened* (vv. 22–23). Sound teaching had been given and careful provision made for the future. There was much to tell at Antioch! (v. 27).

EIGHTH WEEK
From the Life of Paul, Part 2

Sunday: Acts 16:6–15

A step at a time. Here is a good example of step-by-step guidance. (a) *Doors were closed* (vv. 6–8). Only one road was left open to them. (b) *A need was seen* (v. 9), an important element in guidance. God wants his laborers only where there is work for them to do! (c) *The call was obeyed* (v. 10). We can be led on only when we are faithfully following guidance already given. (d) *Opportunities were used* (vv. 13–15). As Paul used the opportunities at hand, God led him on to others.

Monday: Acts 16:16–24

Don't be surprised! Don't be surprised if you learn that lies are being told about you and about your work. If you are a servant of the Lord, you are attacking the very strongholds of Satan, and he will use any means to stop you. The lies told at Philippi (see vv. 20–21) were similar to those in Esther 3:8 and Luke 23:2. After a mock trial (v. 22) the disciples were beaten and cast into prison. What did they do? (See v. 25.) Remember that if Satan can break your spirit, he has won. That's what he is after.

Tuesday: Acts 16:25–34

A simple message. The demon-possessed girl had already testified (v. 17) that Paul and Silas were teaching "the way of salvation." Now the jailer asks what it is (v. 30). See the simple explanation in verse 31. This simple message about Jesus has *plainness* (v. 31)—it is not a complicated philosophy. It has *persuasiveness* (v. 33). The appeal of the Savior's love won the heart of the jailer as it bad that of Lydia (v. 14), It has *power* (v. 34). What a change was wrought in the man's heart that night!

Wednesday: Acts 17: 1–11

Transforming power. "These who have turned the world upside down . . ." (v. 6). Yes, these men had a tremendous effect. Yet it was not they, but the *Word.* Note two things about the Scriptures today. (a) *Preaching out of the Scriptures* (vv. 2–3). Paul opened the Scriptures and demonstrated every point from them. This brought people to Jesus. (b) *Searching into the Scriptures* (v. 11). The Christians who "searched the scriptures daily" were more noble than those who did not. They were built up into instructed, powerful Christians.

Thursday: Acts 18:1–11

"Be not afraid, but speak!" (v. 9). When God's man is in God's place at God's time, he need have no fear. God had sent Paul to Corinth specifically to bring to Christ his chosen ones (v. 10). Until that was accomplished, no man would be permitted to "to hurt" him (v. 10). God's purposes can never be frustrated by sinful men. He always retains control. Paul needed only *boldness to stay* (v. 11), in spite of the opposition and blasphemy; and *boldness to speak* (v. 9), making known God's Word. It is just the same with us.

Friday: Acts 20:17–27

A glimpse into the apostle's heart. Our last two readings from Paul's life show us the springs of love and self-giving that motivated his work. See his gentle heart (v. 19), in spite of his important apostolic position. It was a genuine heart, able to move him to tears in the course of his work. It was generous, sparing nothing in time or effort for the sake of the people (vv. 20–21, 27). It was given utterly to the Lord's service (v. 24); and, as we should certainly expect, it was a glad heart (v. 24).

Saturday: Acts 20:28–38

The Christian worker's responsibilities. The task of the Ephesian elder was primarily spiritual. He held his position, not from men, but from the Spirit of God; and his first responsibility to the people was to feed them (v. 28). He was to watch carefully for error and spiritual dangers (vv. 29–31). With this in mind, he had to know the true Word of God and constantly meditate on it (v. 32). As Paul had been a sound example to the elders at Ephesus, so they were to be the same to their people (vv. 33–35).

NINTH WEEK
The Epistle of the Dedicated Life

Sunday: Philippians 1:1–11

"I have you in my heart" (v. 7). What did Paul have in his heart for the Philippians? (a) *Thankfulness* (vv. 3–5). He remembered the miracles of grace wrought at Philippi (see Acts 16, which we read last week). (b) *Confidence* (vv. 6–7). They were partakers of God's grace, which certainly would be sufficient for their every need. (c) *Prayer* (vv. 9–11). He asked that they might never cease to grow in love, in knowledge of their Lord, and in holiness of living. Thankfulness, confidence, prayer—surely a perfect blend!

Monday: Philippians 1:12–30

"Christ will be magnified" (v. 20). This is really a key verse of the epistle. Its theme is that of a life wholly dedicated to the glory of Christ. See how frequently the name of Christ occurs in this first chapter—it is the center of Paul's thinking. To live is to live for Christ; to die is to be with Christ (vv. 21–23). Everything is for Christ's sake (v. 29). Now notice that this life is the joyous life. Joy is the second theme of the epistle; it springs from the first (vv. 4, 18, 25–26).

Tuesday: Philippians 2:1–18

Serve selflessly! The same theme of dedication is continued from a slightly different standpoint. The dedicated life is one in which self is put last (vv. 3–4). The opening *exhortation* is backed up with the perfect *example*, that of Christ himself (vv. 5 following), who made himself nothing for our sakes. Paul himself is a lesser example of the same (v. 17). Therefore let them give up futile and time-consuming arguments (v. 14), and shine with pure light (v. 15). The outworking of salvation is in service (v. 12).

Wednesday: Philippians 2:19–30

Two faithful workers. Here are two lovely examples of dedicated servants of the Lord. (a) *Timothy*, a man who was willing to be "a good second" to Paul, with no personal ambitions. He was not of those who "seek their own" (v. 21). He had sincere care for young Christians (v. 20). He was willing to be just "a son" to Paul (v. 22). (b) *Epaphroditus*, another loyal helper (v. 25), with no regard for his own life (v. 30), more concerned about the Philippians' anxiety than about his sickness itself! (v. 26). What examples to us!

Thursday: Philippians 3:1–14

"No confidence in the flesh" (v. 3). Paul had passed a vote of no confidence in himself! He had many great advantages in birth, upbringing, and education (vv. 4–6), but all faded into insignificance beside the value of Christ (vv. 7–8) and his righteousness (v. 9). Now the object of his life was to know Christ better (v. 10) and to strive for the perfection and the prize (vv. 11–14). What are you

most proud of about yourself? Birth, education, good looks, voice, brains, or what? Count it loss for Christ.

Friday: Philippians 3:15–4:5

Life lived in the Lord. Paul had said, "To me, to live is Christ" (1:21). But what did it mean in practice? Here are three examples: (a) *Stand fast in the Lord* (4:1). Resist Satan's onslaughts against your faith. Christ is coming (3:20); meanwhile trust him. (b) *Be of the same mind in the Lord* (4:2). Paul said, "Imitate me" (3:17). Well, what was his attitude to fellow Christians? (4:1). (c) *Rejoice in the Lord* (4:4). Keep thinking of the Lord Jesus, his power, and his coming. Let him fill your life with his joy.

Saturday: Philippians 4:6–23

Secrets of inner peace. Here are the secrets: (a) *Let prayer be constant* (vv. 6–7). Bring every anxiety to God and leave it with him. (b) *Let thoughts be pure* (vv. 8–9). Avoid situations that draw your thoughts into godless paths. (c) *Let little be enough* (vv. 12–13). There is no peace when the heart is restlessly longing for more; find your all in Christ. (d) *Let God be trusted* (v. 19). Not all your wants, 'tis true, but all your need shall be supplied.

TENTH WEEK
Treasures from the Psalms

Sunday: Psalm 57

"God most high" (v. 2). The key theme of this psalm tells how wonderful God is for the believer in all circumstances. Notice *the believer's trouble* (v. 1). He is not shielded from normal adversities because he must show

God to be all-sufficient. Where is *the believer's trust?* Verses 2 and 3 will give the answer. The believer knows that God cannot fail and will never let him down. Then see *the believer's triumph* (vv. 7–11). He can sing a hymn of praise and thanksgiving even before his prayers are answered. This is because he believes in God. It is a triumph of faith.

Monday: Psalm 62

Where are you looking? Eve sinned as a result of looking at the wrong person and the wrong thing. Where you look can make a big difference. David *looked away* (vv. 9–10) from human strength and human riches. Never make the mistake of thinking that many people and much money mean a strong work for God. David *looked up* (v. 1) to God. He waited to know God's will. He found all his power in his Lord (v. 11). And, of course, he *looked ahead* to an assured future of safety and service (vv. 2, 5–6).

Tuesday: Psalm 66

"I will declare what He has done" (v. 16). This is another psalm that shows glory shining through a troubled life. The Psalmist and his people had suffered greatly for their faith in the Lord (vv. 11–12). But he realized that it was God himself who *brought them into* affliction so that he might bring them out into a richer experience (vv. 11–12). And the purpose behind it? Verse 10 speaks of the refining action of trouble. Faith's silver is purified. And verse 16 reminds us that others are blessed through the tested saint's witness.

Wednesday: Psalm 84

The soul's first love (v. 2). This beautiful psalm is all about the believer as a lover. His whole being cries out for the One he adores, his living God. He longs for his Master's company, and to dwell all his life in the Lord's presence (vv. 4, 10). Through spending time with him, meditating upon him, and telling him of your love, you will find that love deepened in your heart. And out of that communion will come grace, glory, and good things (v. 11). You will go from strength to strength (v. 7). Is your love for him increasing daily?

Thursday: Psalm 86

"Unite my heart" (v. 11). David feared *the enemy within* more than *the enemy without,* his own divided heart more than the proud and violent men. So the first and longest portion of this psalm is a prayer for *inward strength* (vv. 1–13). He felt his spiritual poverty (v. 1) and his ignorance of God's way for him (v. 11). This is the kind of prayer the Lord delights to answer (v. 7). Only then did David ask for *outward strength* (vv. 14–17). God is not so remote that he is not concerned about our circumstances! Try him and see!

Friday: Psalm 91

What promises! This psalm is full of promises—almost every verse contains one. Physical safety is the theme; the saint's physical life is in the Lord's hands. He need not fear *disease* (vv. 3, 6); God knows its sources and controls them. No *terror* need disturb his slumbers at night (v. 5), for God does not sleep. Even war cannot pluck the saint from God's hands (v. 5). And while we must always take proper care and precaution, no *accident* can happen; nothing that comes is an accident with God (vv. 11–12). See John 10:28 for the best fulfillment of verse 16.

Saturday: Psalm 96

Open your mouth! Here are three things to do with your mouth (a) *Sing*! (vv. 1–2). The Lord loves to hear his people singing. But let your songs be about him and his salvation. (b) *Worship*! (vv. 7–9). We are tempted to think that activity is a substitute for worship, but what does this psalm teach? (c) *Speak*! (v. 10). Singing with the saints and worship in the sanctuary must lead to witness to the sinners. We must tell two things: the coming judgment of the Lord (vv. 10, 13) and the joy of knowing his salvation (vv. 11–12).

ELEVENTH WEEK
A Venture of Faith

Sunday: Nehemiah 1:1–11

God calls a leader. How does he do it? In Nehemiah's case there are three steps mentioned. *Step One*: Nehemiah's heart was stirred. If your heart is not burdened at the thought of those without Christ, you are not ready to be a Christian leader (v. 4). *Step Two:* Nehemiah poured out his soul in prayer. Leadership must be born in the experience of prayer. Notice the humility, yet the urgency, of his requests (vv. 6, 10). *Step Three*: Nehemiah tried the door! He tried to take what would be the natural first step, to see whether this was really God's leading (v. 11).

Monday: Nehemiah 2:1–8

"The good hand of my God" (v. 8). Consider these aspects of Nehemiah's life: (a) *His boldness.* It was not rashness. See how respectful and courteous he was in verses 3, 5, 7.

But even fear did not keep him from speaking (v. 2). (b) *His prayer* (v. 4). He lived in a spirit of prayer each moment. Prayer in the secret place (1:4) led to prayer in time of need. He attributed success to God's answer to his prayer (v. 8). (c) *His faith.* "I set him a time" (v. 6). Sure now that God was working, he had enough faith to set the king a time limit!

Tuesday: Nehemiah 2:9–20

Prudence and tact. Nehemiah wanted to be sure of the situation before he took any action. Hence his night inspection of the ruins, telling no one of his purpose (vv. 12, 16). Do not rush into hasty action without being in full possession of the facts; you will only end up with regrets. Notice also Nehemiah's discrimination in his choice of companions. He enlisted the support of the spiritual leaders of the community who would get the people behind them. But he refused the help of the crafty enemies of the Jews. He attached little importance to mere numbers.

Wednesday: Nehemiah 4:1–14

Wise answers. God gave Nehemiah wisdom as difficulties began to arise. (a) *The answer to mockery.* Scoffers always dog the footsteps of God's servants. Nehemiah's answer was to continue in prayer and to ignore the jests (vv. 1–6). (b) *The answer to threats.* As mockery fails, more serious measures are contemplated by the foes. The answer is still to pray and to take protective steps (vv. 7–9). (c) *The answer to despair.* Constant, nagging opposition can wear down faith and lead to despondency. The answer? "Remember the Lord!" (See vv. 10–14.)

Thursday: Nehemiah 4:15–23

"Our God will fight for us" (v. 20). Nehemiah was a good leader. He led his people's faith away from himself to God. God and his purposes are constantly mentioned by Nehemiah. But at the same time Nehemiah taught the people how to organize themselves properly, and he was a wise and careful planner. He did not believe that to be spiritual meant to be disorganized. See also how Nehemiah led the people rather than pushing them. He took his share of the hard work and would be in the forefront of any battle that might develop.

Friday: Nehemiah 6:1–9

"I am doing a great work" (v. 3). The work God has given you to do, however small it may seem to be, is "a great work"; and any direction away from it is "down" (v. 3). Say "No" to anything in your environment that would weaken your hands (v. 9) in the work you are sure God has given you to do. Do not be led astray. Be persistent in your refusals (v. 4)—do not let constant suggestion weaken your resolve. Do not fear misunderstanding or misrepresentation (vv. 6–7). Above all, seek the strength that God gives so that you may do a firstclass job.

Saturday: Nehemiah 6:10–16

"Should such a man as I flee?" (v. 11). Notice two facts: (a) *A final test.* The devil is not one to give up halfway. He will test the servant of God right to the end. If he can spoil the man, he has spoiled the work. Nehemiah was always watchful so that he might recognize Satan's attacks (v. 12). (b) *A finished task.* "So the wall was finished" (v. 15). God had given Nehemiah a work to do, and he persevered until

it was finished. God needs such men and women today. The Lord himself is the perfect example (see John 17:4).

TWELFTH WEEK
Secrets of Fruitful Discipleship

Sunday: John 14:12–27

What privileges! What a privileged person the Christian believer is! Here we see that he has (a) *a wonderful promise* (v. 12). If he has real faith, he shall do greater works even than those of Christ himself in his days on earth. He also has (b) a *wonderful Presence* (vv. 17, 20, 23). Father, Son, and Holy Spirit, all three, take up their abode in him—a permanent dwelling, not an occasional visit. And the believer has (c) *a wonderful peace* (v. 27), for the promise and the presence will take away all anxiety. What a heritage we have!

Monday: John 15:1–11

The vine and the branches. If you are a true Christian, you are a branch of "the true vine," Christ. *Your calling* is to bear fruit (v. 2). A vine bears fruit through its branches; but the branches can do nothing on their own (v. 5). They must stay in contact with the stem. *Your need,* therefore, is to abide in Christ—consciously live in fellowship with him day by day (v. 4). You will then be fruitful in your Christian life. *Your object* in all this is to bring glory to the divine husbandman or gardener (vv. 1, 8). Fine fruit brings credit to the grower!

Tuesday: John 15:12–19

The forgotten commandment (v. 17). Here is an order we

are bound to obey: we must love every fellow Christian. Only if we do so, do we count as friends of Christ (v. 14). (a) *The power of love declared.* We are *together* to bear fruit, in the loving unity of the Church (vv. 12, 16). It is difficult for one branch to bear fruit unless all the others do! (b) *The power of love demonstrated.* The disciples were about to see the love of Christ redeeming the world (vv. 12–13). Only love could give us the cross; only love can bring men to it.

Wednesday: John 16:1–14

Be prepared! Jesus Christ tells us what life will be like for us while he is away. (a) *Our deadly foes* (v. 2). Life will not be easy. Why will so many people oppose us if we are living for Christ (v. 3)? And why does Jesus tell us about it here (v. 4)? It is a great comfort to know that it is all allowed for in God's plan. (b) *Our divine friend* (v. 7). The Holy Spirit is our never failing and never departing friend. He will support our witness (vv. 8–11), will be our guide (v. 13), and best of all will teach us of Jesus (v. 14).

Thursday: John 17: 1–8

"Glory!" (v. 5). Glory is the theme of these verses. It comes through union with God the Father (v. 5) and is supremely seen in acts of pure self-sacrifice such as Christ's death on the cross. It comes from God; but as it is shown forth on earth, it is enriched. Thus the Father himself is freshly glorified by it (vv. 1, 4). What God gave to Jesus is available to us also (vv. 6–8); therefore, we ourselves may be glorified and may glorify God (see 2 Corinthians 3:18 and 1 Corinthians 6:20). Is your life glorious?

Friday: John 17:9–17

Christ prays for you and me. The deep love of Christ for his own breathes through these verses. What does he ask his Father to do for us? (a) *"Keep them!"* (v. 15). God gave us to Christ to be his people; now Christ hands us back to the Father for safekeeping (v. 11). How safe we are in the hands of our God! (See John 10:29.) (b) *"Sanctify them!"* (v. 17). Christ's longing is that we might share his own complete holiness; yet evil is so powerful (v. 15). We must know God's Word if Christ's prayer is to be answered (v. 17).

Saturday: John 17:18–26

Sent out by Christ. We Christians are sent out into the world just as Christ was sent down at Bethlehem (v. 18). What does this involve? (a) *Responsibilities.* We have the responsibility of holiness (v. 19) and of brotherly unity (vv. 21–23). We must speak Christ's Word (v. 20). (b) *Privileges.* We share Christ's own privileges of sonship. We have a share in God's glory (v. 22) and the same unchanging love from the Father that Christ had (v. 26). We are "one" with Christ in God (v. 21). Praise God! What a life is ours!

BIBLIOGRAPHY

Baxter, J. Sidlow. *Does God Still Guide?* Zondervan, 1971.

Carlson, Dwight. *Living God's Will.* Revell, 1976.

Elliot, Elisabeth. *A Slow and Certain Light.* Word Books, 1976.

Howard, J. Grant. *Knowing God's Will—And Doing It.* Zondervan, 1976.

Kunz, Marilyn. *Patterns for Living with God.* InterVarsity, 1970.

Little, Paul. *Affirming the Will of God.* InterVarsity, 1976.

Redpath, A. *Getting to Know the Will of God.* InterVarsity, 1976.

Tucker, Michael R. *Live Confidently, How to Know God's Will.* Tyndale, 1975.

Weatherhead, Leslie. *The Will of God.* Abingdon, 1976.

Weiss, G. Christian. *The Perfect Will of God.* Moody, 1950.

Philippians 4:13
Chapter 7

Psalm 37:23
Chapter 4

Psalm 32:8
Chapter 1

Romans 12:1–2
Chapter 8

Proverbs 3:5–6
Chapter 5

1 John 2:17
Chapter 2

1 Corinthians 10:31
Chapter 9

1 Peter 2:21

2 Corinthians 13:5
Chapter 3

I will instruct thee and teach thee in the way which thou shalt go: I will guide thee with mine eye.

The steps of a good man are ordered by the LORD: and he delighteth in his way.

I can do all things through Christ which strengtheneth me.

And the world passeth away, and the lust thereof; but he that doeth the will of God abideth forever.

Trust in the LORD with all thine heart; and lean not unto thine own understanding.
In all thy ways acknowledge him, and he shall direct thy paths.

I beseech you therefore, brethren, by the mercies of God, that ye present your bodies a living sacrifice, holy, acceptable unto God, which is your reasonable service.
And be ye not conformed to this world: but be ye transformed by the renewing of your mind, that ye may prove what is that good, and acceptable, and perfect will of God.

Examine yourselves, whether ye be in the faith; prove your own selves. Know ye not your own selves, how that Jesus Christ is in you, except ye be reprobates?

For even hereunto were ye called: because Christ also suffered for us, leaving us an example, that ye should follow his steps.

Whether therefore ye eat, or drink, or whatsoever ye do, do all to the glory of God.

Titus 2:11–12

Hebrews 10:23–24

Ephesians 3:20–21

For the grace of God that bringeth salvation hath appeared to all men,

Teaching us that, denying ungodliness and worldly lusts, we should live soberly, righteously, and godly in this present world.

Let us hold fast the profession of our faith without wavering; (for he is faithful that promised;)

And let us consider one another to provoke unto love and to good works.

Now unto him that is able to do exceeding abundantly above all that we ask or think, according to the power that worketh in us,

Unto him be glory in the church by Christ Jesus throughout all ages, world without end. Amen.